Killers & Boosters

for

Child Custody Cases

(Attitude Adjustment for Child Custody Litigants)

Compiled by

Charlotte Hardwick

ISBN 1-58747-043-8

The publisher may be contacted at:

Pale Horse Publishing

T (800) 646-5590 (936) 327-1104

PaleHorsePublishing.com

P.O. Box 1255 Livingston, Texas 77351-1255 U.S.A.

Dedication

I watched you in amazement.
Unable to believe anyone could be so lovely and perfect.
To my astonishment now there are two of you.

Emptiness existed
before you came into my life.
I was unaware of the void.
However, I am aware of the fullness that exists now.
Thank you with all my heart.

for Kelly and Bethany

Introduction

Educators and other professionals see well-adjusted, secure, and confident children when those children are supported by two parents (married or not, living together or not) committed to their care and upbringing.

Non-custodial parenting does not equal bad parenting, any more than custodial parenting guarantees good parenting. Just as all non-custodial fathers are not deadbeat dads, not all non-custodial mothers are unfit mothers. Some of us have lost custody of children in court cases and some of us have voluntarily given up custody. How, where and with whom children live should not define the non-custodial parent as less than.

In 1991 I was forced into the custody case arena. I began looking for 'The Answer'. I wanted to know what the mediators, evaluators, and judges wanted to hear. I was willing to paint myself yellow if that is what they wanted. I do not even look good in yellow.

After years of working with thousands of other parents in parents' rights groups, child protective service agencies in nine major cities, attending seminars with counselors and psychologists and interviewing attorneys, judges, mediators and guardian ad litems; reading many books on custody and writing several of my own I have found out that there is no "the answer".

Our cases, lives, children, communities and the laws that affect us vary to such a huge degree that there are too many answers. This book deals with what others do to us, what we do to ourselves; love, pain, fear, the past, present, and future, perception and perspective. There is no 'The Answer'. This is not a book of legal advice or pat answers just a book of suggestions and options. Use what you can and ignore the rest.

Disclaimer

The Small Print: This resource is for information and discussion purposes only. It isn't meant to be legal advice and you shouldn't treat it as such. If you want legal advice, speak with a lawyer familiar with your state's laws who can review "all" of the facts and the law applicable to your situation.

Although the author and publisher have exhaustively researched all sources to ensure the accuracy and completeness of the information contained in this book, they assume no responsibility for errors, inaccuracies, omissions, or any inconsistency herein. They assume no liability or responsibility for the use or misuse of the information contained in this book.

Readers should use their own judgment or consult an attorney for specific applications to their individual problems.

This book does not contain legal advice. This book is designed to provide information about the subject matter covered. It is sold with the understanding that the publisher and author are not engaged in rendering legal, or other professional services.

The message of this book is to be prepared and to know there is an element of chance in the way your behavior will be seen by others. However, this book will greatly improve your ability to be the kind of parent you want to be.

Reviews

Like chicken soup for the custody case, **Killers & Boosters**, gave me a place to get some perspective. Like chicken soup, you can take some whenever you need it. It couldn't hurt and probably, it will help. Nash Raeside, LI, NY

I was handling my custody case like a diet. I would read a book and use that system until the results seemed too slow or complicated, then dive into yet another (book). I was frustrated and exhausted. **Killers & Boosters,** helped me use the positive points from all I have learned and even profit from my failures. Jim Newman, Miami, FL

Advice is usually given with the right intention at the wrong time. To make things worse, most advice givers are offended when you do not jump to do what they tell you to do. **Killers & Boosters** offers you advice when you want it and are ready to hear it. You can act on what you have learned, mull it over or discard the advice all together without interference. Jan Harrison, Arlington, VA

I carry **Killers & Boosters** in my briefcase. I read it in low moments and feel recharged. It inspired me to overcome the negative thoughts I had been allowing myself to have. It reminded me of my gains and what is truly important in life. James Gourmand, Billings, MT

My brother sent me this book. The brother who never talked about his feelings. I know **Killers & Boosters** is his way of saying the tough and the supportive things he can't put a voice to. This little book really helped me. Don Marine, Lancaster, PA

I needed something to bring me back from the crushing lows and unreliable highs that have thrashed my emotions for the past two years. The sub-title, **Attitude Adjustment for Custody Case Litigants**, has given me a touchstone to reality and helped me with a real attitude adjustment. Clive Friedman, Upper Sandusky, Ohio

Killers & Boosters is just what I needed. Cynthiana West, Anderson, IN

My kids loved Killers & Boosters as much as I did. Lots to think about in a little book. I found my attitude did need adjustment. My kids helped me see through some of my blind spots. I have taped 3" X 5" cards with some of this advice around the house. P.E. Foret, Nashville, TN

Some of this information I already knew, but hadn't considered in this situation. Most of this advice I had never heard at all. Until **Killers & Boosters** made things clear, I was not using any advice correctly. I laughed, cried, nodded and was puzzled as to why I hadn't seen most of this myself. Now the fog is cleared and I can proceed. Ralph Sprague, Berkley, CA

I have all the books by this author. This small volume is huge on 'Right Think,' especially, when the people you love encourage you to 'Wrong Think'. It's amazing how vindictive your family and friends get when you are wronged. The instant pleasure of revenge is quickly replaced by pain you feel when you see the damage you have done to your own case. **Killers & Boosters** keeps you on the right path. Money well spent. Jackie Runge, Palm Springs, CA

Lots of help from a little bitty book! Don't expect **Killers & Boosters** to solve all the problems you are having with your ex. It can't. It can help you adjust your attitude to better deal with the situations as they arise. I loved it. I shared it. I even give it as a gift to others going through the same things. I highly recommend it for what it is. Nothing more and nothing less. It gave me hope and a new attitude that has helped when nothing else did. Read it, you'll see. Jodi Lincon Firebird Lake, AZ

I love this kind of book. **Killers & Boosters** is made up of short quotes and statements to make you think about what is really happening it's inexpensive and it helps. Amazon Reader

About the Compiler

Since 1991, Charlotte Hardwick has written seven books dealing with child custody. Her work brings a fresh view to the situations faced by children, parents, grandparents, stepparents and the people who care about them.

Charlotte's ability to offer innovative new options for common problems as well as situation specific alternatives is a gift to those lost in pain, anger and defeat. Her personal custody success was eclipsed by the experience gained since 1992 in hands on research, and interaction with parents, attorneys, judges, psychologists, mediators, guidance counselors, law enforcement, activists, legislators and adult children of child custody disputes.

The calming effect her books produce is as comforting as holding a friend's hand. Many of the processes are explained in a step-by-step manner with many examples.

The information is empowering and healing. Charlotte has been a frequent speaker at parent's rights groups and professional business organizations. Human resource professionals are acutely aware of how a custody battle negatively affects an employee and can even reduce the production of other closely related employees with whom they interact.

Charlotte's work can shorten the time-line of the initial custody battle, reduce the costs considerably, and minimize the long-term negative effects for the children, employee, family and employer.

Books by Charlotte include:

Win Your Child Custody War

Witness Guide (for deposition or court)

Dear Judge, (Children's letters to the judge)

Case Management Forms (for Child Custody Cases)

Killers & Boosters (for Child Custody Cases)

Long Distance Parenting

How to Use This Book

You are unique from any other person on earth. Your custody experience will be different from anyone elses, no matter how hard lawyers and the courts try to push you into an established mold and attempt to impose accepted attitudes and feelings. No one will feel or even understand what you feel.

This is a unique book compiled especially for you. You will get as much out of it as you put into it! You can read the whole book in a couple of hours and learn a little.

OR

You can take the time to read and think about each listing.

First, decide if the listing has anything to do with what you are experiencing. If it doesn't, go on to the next.

If it does apply to something you are experiencing, think about what the listing is saying to you. Take the time to see if there is some new way for you to see an incident, your situation, or the other party.

Above all, be very truthful with yourself. Allow yourself to step back. Look at incidents and situations from your child's point of view, the point of view of the other parent, the point of view of the court, and the point of view of the long-term impact of what is happening.

Often your instincts are affirmed by the listing. Sometimes, a listing will challenge the way you have been handling a situation.

The listing may help you understand why someone is behaving in a particular manner. The listing may help you change your life in a way that will make this process easier.

This is not a big life-changing program. It is small tips, bits, ideas that can help you NOW!

Parents who have this book say it has made them a new and different person when dealing with the stresses of a child custody case.

Remember, it is your choice as to what you want to do with your case, and only you can change it. That is, IF you really want to. Many, many people want things to change but don't want to change themselves. Why should they? They have so many people feeling sorry for them!

We all learned when we were small children that to get attention all we had to do was cry or sulk and we would get attention! Well, many of us are still in that old way of thinking! Have you fallen into that trap?

If you have the courage to change how you see things and what you can do about them, you can. This can be your first step.

This simple book was compiled to offer you some new ways to see and think about what is happening at this time in your life.

Killers & Busters for Custody Cases

Attitude Adjustment for Child Custody Litigants

1. This is not about you. It is about your child. Always.
2. No amount of money or expert legal wrangling will advance your chances of winning custody of your child as quickly as the other parent's stupidity.
3. Action is the Antidote.
4. Courts may truly be said to have neither FORCE nor WILL, but merely judgment. Sir William Blackstone
5. Each day of our lives, we make deposits in the memory banks of our children. Charles R. Swindoll
6. Love should be a verb.

7. Court was not designed to give you justice; it was designed to render a decision in accordance with the existing law.
8. The greatest "gift" that two divorced people can give to their kids: Don't blame each other any more for the hurts you caused each other.
9. Establish a positive working partnership with the other parent that is visible to your child. If you are not able to create and maintain a happy association, at the very least, build a polite partnership.
10. Never accept empty promises, get it in writing, accept a friend's help when you can, and learn to do without it.
11. The greatest test of courage on earth is to bear defeat without losing heart. Robert Green Ingersoll
12. Sometimes, it is more important to discover what one cannot do, than what one can do. Lin Yutang
13. Tears are not a sign of weakness. They are usually a sign of physical or emotional pain. Tears are better released than stored.
14. Two individuals living apart will have more expenses than two individuals living together.
15. Keep a detailed log or diary for an extended length of time, even if things are going well. You may need to refer to what was happening yesterday, a year or two from now.
16. Do not lose the focus of your goals by allowing yourself to be suckered in by a heightened degree of suffering.
17. If you become aware that your child is experiencing emotional difficulties because of this custody case, get professional help right away.
18. Rudeness is the weak person's imitation of strength.
19. Do not move your home more often than necessary.
20. The pain of leaving those you grow to love is only the prelude to understanding yourself and others.

21. The angry man will defeat himself in battle as well as in life. Samurai Maxim
22. The courts were established to protect the laws. The laws were established to protect the people. You cannot change the court. You can change the law.
23. I will expect my children to respect other children and all family members. I will not allow put downs or unkind remarks in my home.
24. Almost everything comes from almost nothing. Frederic Amiel
25. Love is the condition in which the happiness of another person is essential to your own. Robert A. Heinlein
26. We worry about what a child will be tomorrow, yet we forget that he is someone today. Stacia Tauscher
27. To know others is wisdom, to know oneself is enlightenment. Tao Te Ching
28. Do not jump to conclusions if there appears to be a problem. Ask if what you think was said, was in fact, what was meant by repeating the statement.
29. Consider sharing rather than alternating holidays.
30. Tell the children that the separation is going to take place before it takes place, and tell the children together.
31. Parents often can interview the child to get content for audio/video tape that a child can cherish forever.
32. You know it is a bad day when the only person you do not want to know what is going on, is the only one listening.
33. Where there is a way into a problem, there is a way out. Not a way we might want to take, but a way none the less.
34. It's a funny thing about life; if you refuse to accept anything but the best, very often you get it. Somerset Maugham
35. Instant availability without continuous presence is probably the most important position a parent can play.

36. Old rule in child custody disputes: anger does not win.
37. Remove the words *"should, I should have, I should never have"* from your vocabulary and mind. Guilt grows from this kind of negative thinking. First, forgive yourself of all the old *should-a's*. Second, whenever you feel the bitter taste of *should*, take the steps necessary to respond the way you really want to or do the things you feel necessary.
38. One person's justice is another person's injustice.
39. Choose your words and actions carefully when dealing with the other parent. They are your children's true inheritance. Vicki Lansky
40. Search for more possibilities.
41. Encourage your children to give thought to how they will solve a problem. Tell them when they have done a good job of planning, even if they did not come up with the desired results.
42. You display your character best when you describe others.
43. The horrific torture inflicted by the medieval system has been replaced by cross-examination in court.
44. Work things out together with the other parent and let your children be part of the process.
45. Children need and want stability, schedules help.
46. As an example of the fact that there are many right ways to do something: Each of the days of the week is designated as the Sabbath for some nationality or religion. Sunday is the Christian, Monday the Greek, Tuesday the Persian, Wednesday the Assyrian, Thursday the Egyptian, Friday the Turkish, and Saturday the Jewish.
47. Be better than your reputation.
48. You can't control others, you can't control most events, you can only do your best. Do your best.

49. It is common sense to take a method and try it. If it fails, admit it frankly and try another. Above all, try something. Former US President Franklin D. Roosevelt

50. Do the right thing. It will gratify some people and astonish the rest. Mark Twain

51. For every problem, there is one solution, which is simple, neat and wrong. H.L. Mencken

52. You may be wrong in your opinions, but do not be wrong in your facts.

53. What words could be said to you today that would give you the greatest joy? I love you. Give that to your child.

54. Prove all things; hold fast that which is good. 1 Thessalonians 5:21

55. People are too quick to dismiss the pain of others, especially that which they inflict.

56. If time and money were no object, what would I choose to be doing?

57. When you are feeling sad, sing. You start with sad songs and progress to happy ones. It is hard to stay sad when you are singing.

58. Present a united front with the other parent in the handling of any problems with the children.

59. Be sure to include a sense of humor when you pack your survival kit.

60. Your children are not your children. They are the sons and daughters of Life's longing for itself. They come through you but not from you, though they are with you, and yet they belong not to you. You may give them your love, but not your thoughts. For they have their own thoughts. You may house their bodies but not their souls, for their souls dwell in the house of tomorrow, which you cannot visit, not even in your dreams. You may strive to be like them, but seek not to make them like you. For life goes nor backward, not tarries with yesterday. Kahlil Gibran, the Prophet

61. You cannot make everything right. Someone tried.
62. You can best see yourself when looking into the eyes of your child.
63. Make it possible for your children to celebrate dates important to the other parent, such as birthdays, anniversaries, religious holidays, etc. It may be necessary at times to remind the children to acknowledge these occasions, perhaps by helping your children purchase or make cards or gifts.
64. Send the other parent some of your child's school papers that you usually put on the refrigerator door!
65. Too fast, old. Too slow, smart.
66. Sometimes, divorce is a symptom of dysfunctional peoples' lives, not the cause.
67. If the other parent is determined to engage you in a protracted custody battle, pray they find honest, competent, equitable help. The alternative will make things much worse for you.
68. Life is only ours on loan.
69. Do not permit the children to have too much decision-making power in adult matters.
70. If it won't look good if you get caught, don't do it!
71. Do not scream at your children. It makes them scream back, and they do not want to be screamers. Big screamers and little screamers sound awful.
72. Be sensitive to the children's needs as well as your own.
73. Plan for and consult with the other parent in advance of the client's or other parent's time with the children.
74. Success and happiness are not achieved by the absence of conflict, but the ability to cope with it.
75. Praise is habit forming.
76. I thought the pastor who pronounced us married was a wonderful man. I know the judge that pronounced us divorced was a saint.

77. Be flexible with regard to visitation times if you are the custodial parent.

78. When things do not go right, do not over react. Most challenges can be handled in more than one way. Decide the problem is no big deal and choose another way to deal with it.

79. Wrong is wrong. Even if it helps you.

80. Do not worry about the clothes and toys that go to the child's other home and do not return. Your child still has the use of the things you have purchased. After all that is why you bought the items.

81. Your child custody case must be more than a pile of information. In order to win, it must be a pattern of information arranged in a particular way.

82. Your children's feelings are more important to you than you being right or proving the other parent wrong.

83. The professional may apologize for the fact that all the information offered seems useless and then charge you for an hour of time. Find something in it you can use.

84. Love the part of your child, that is the other parent.

85. Be great in your actions, as you have been in your thoughts. Suit the action to the work and the work to the action. Shakespeare

86. Just when you think your child raising work is done, you become a grandparent.

87. There is so much good in the worst of us, and so much bad in the best of us, that it hardly becomes any one of us to talk about the rest of us.

88. Help your child enjoy the things the other parent does and buys for the child. Remove any guilt the child has about this small happiness. Let the child know, "We all love you and want you to have nice things and nice experiences in both families."

89. You can do something in an instant that will give you heartache for life.

90. Discard old negative ways of dealing with this person. Extend the respect and patience you would a new acquaintance that shares your love for these children.
91. Do not judge every action the other parent makes as good or bad. It wastes your time and even God does not judge a person until the end of his or her days.
92. Send your favorite family cookies or other food items with recipes and the family story behind them.
93. Do not give your children everything they ask for. Sometimes, they are just testing you to see how much they can get.
94. Identify and use reliable, unbiased witnesses.
95. Encourage the children's good feelings about the other parent and the extended family on both sides.
96. Show your appreciation for the support others give you. Do not be embarrassed to express the value you place upon their efforts.
97. Don't make children hate. Hate is a boomerang.
98. Be careful before committing your actions to the teachings of an eye for an eye. It may leave you blind.
99. Have your child accompany you to buy a flowering bush or tree (as your yard or patio space allows). As a team, you can plant and fertilize it. Each time the child is with you the ritual of caring for the project will be something you do together. It will anchor the child to your home, and to you while the child is away from you. Your child will think of you whenever your child sees the same plant elsewhere.
100. Write stories for your children of family past, history, family members, deceased family members, and your childhood. Include photographs when possible.
101. The ability to endure hardship patiently is a great virtue and will bring you maturity, stability, and spiritual strength.
102. Be aware of behavioral changes in your child.

103. Let your children do as much for themselves as they can. That is how they learn. If you do everything for them, they will never be able to do anything for themselves.

104. When your needs overwhelm you, look around and find one with greater need to assist. This is one of the best kinds of rest break.

105. Take the children to a therapist if the psychological adjustment appears to be too problematic.

106. If there is a matter of disagreement, work out that problem, without adding new points to the discussion. Do not insert or allow the other side to insert any old arguments. Address the matter at hand in a manner that will allow settlement. Offer several acceptable options.

107. What you do about what they do, is more important than what they do. Dr. James Papen

108. We win justice quickest by rendering justice to the other party. Gandhi

109. The way to get appreciation from your children later, is to show them how you express it to others now.

110. Be responsive to others, not responsible for others.

111. When you are wrong about something, admit it. It will not hurt your children's opinion of you. Additionally, it will make it easier for your children to admit it when they are wrong.

112. Success is where preparation meets opportunity.

113. One benefit of a college education is that it helps you worry more intelligently about your custody case.

114. Avoid misunderstandings during verbal communication, restate the information given to you before you answer or give your information.

115. Doing what you like is freedom. Liking what you do is happiness.

116. Find small magic moments in everyday things you do with your child.

117. Provide the children with an emotional environment in which they are free to continue to love the other parent and to spend time with that parent.

118. Give your child a loving nickname; something the child likes. Avoid put down names like Shorty or Slow Poke. Find nice names like Fast Feet, Princess or Star Man.

119. Give thought to the choices before you and make the best choice you can. Do not regret choices made. Focus on a positive direction.

120. Be open and free with your affirmation of the achievements and positive actions of your child. Do not criticize. There are many right ways to do things.

121. Camp out with your child. If you live too far from the woods or cannot get time away, camp in the back yard.

122. Children do and should love both parents.

123. Tell the children as often as necessary that you still love them and that you are not getting divorced from them.

124. Think about how happy you would be if you lost everything you have right now and then got it back again.

125. Progress comes in “can”, stagnation in “cannot.”

126. What sunshine is to flowers, a child’s smiles are to parents. They are but fleeting, to be sure. But scattered along the pathway of life the good they do is incredible.

127. Do not let the fear inside of you make you turn and run away. Stevie Nicks

128. Do not tell lies in front of your children or ask them to lie. It makes them think less of you and less of themselves, even if they are supposed to be doing you a favor.

129. Always leave your children with loving words. Make sure that the things they see you do and the things they hear you say reflect the real you. Do not let them see your inappropriate reaction to another person’s inappropriate behavior or words. It may be the last time you see your children.

130. It takes a long time to become the person you really want to be.

131. Set backs are set-ups, for comebacks.

132. Is what you want from this custody case within the range of probable outcomes? Is your position clearly supported by the facts and the rules of law?

133. Love is the only reality; fear is something we conjure up in our minds.

134. Do not compare your children with others, especially if the comparison will hurt somebody's feelings. They do not want to be considered smarter than others because it will hurt other people's feelings. They do not want to be considered dumber because it will hurt.

135. We are responsible for what we do, no matter how we feel.

136. Confidence is the feeling you have before you really understand the problem.

137. Anger can be a useful tool to send us in some better direction, or, if misdirected, it can be a tool for our own self-destruction. Alternatively, it can be something that in some cases can be simply dissipated, overwhelming the bitterness of anger with the sweetness of a better life, making the anger trivial. Revenge, is a stupid waste of time, except when honoring the old phrase "living well is the best revenge". On the other hand, anger needs to be resolved. You decide the best way to resolve yours. I suggest gaining revenge by living well.

138. Forgiveness is letting what was, be. What is now, be. What will be, come.

139. You are always free to change your mind and choose a different future or a different past.

140. Do not be offended by negative feedback. Turn it into positive action.

141. Children will have feelings of powerlessness and helplessness.

142. In disagreements, deal only with the current situation. Do not bring up the past.

143. We are continually faced by great opportunities brilliantly disguised as insoluble problems. Lee Iacocca

144. Express affection many ways verbally, physically, and emotionally. Express your feelings in loving words like, "I love you," "I like the kind of person you are," and, "I think you are a very special child." Be physically affectionate. Lavish your child with hugs and kisses. Cuddle your child while reading a story or watching television. Sit together while playing, hold hands while walking, or work closely together on a project.

145. Time is nature's way of keeping everything from happening all at once.

146. Two wrongs are only the beginning.

147. Take some time to think about anything negative that has happened. Try to analyze the entire matter and identify any actions you took that effected the situation adversely. Prepare an alternative and more constructive course of action in the event you are placed in a similar spot again.

148. Praying helps.

149. Be the parent and allow your child to be a child.

150. Those who say you can accomplish anything you set your mind to, have never before been to a custody court hearing.

151. All issues of separation, divorce and custody must be determined for the well-being of your children.

152. The best relationship is one in which your love for each other exceeds your need for each other.

153. As contagion of sickness makes sickness, contagion of trust can make trust. Marianne Moore

154. Children are never detached spectators when their parents fight. Learn to restrain yourself to protect your children.

155. Success always occurs in private, and failure in full view.

156. Do not always be giving orders. If you suggest something instead of giving a command, your children will do it faster.

157. Be active. Not inactive!

158. You must not act out of anger, guilt, fear, greed, revenge, and desire to punish or control the other parent.

159. Parents hold their children's hands for just a short while and their hearts forever.

160. If you recognize the warning signs and cannot win custody; you may need an attorney to assist you in getting the most liberal visitation possible. Watch out for the words Minimum Visitation or Visitation Guidelines. Minimum means you can get more. Guidelines are just that, only guidelines.

161. Understand and live within the limitations of what is possible.

162. Say "Thank you" to the other parent. Even if the children were picked up late, did not bring everything home they took with them and have not been fed dinner yet.

163. You can keep going long after you cannot.

164. Be proactive. Not reactive.

165. Children do not get much mail and they love getting unusual packages. Create oversized letters, collages, things that have to be mailed in a mailing tube. Include small gifts: a package of garden seeds, a coupon to a fast food restaurant, some bath powder and other similar items.

166. Children are not mind readers. Talk to them.

167. It is the job of the opposing lawyer to attempt to impugn your integrity, by making attacks. It is your job not to rise to the bait by yelling back. Stay quiet and answer as if you knew for sure that if the opposing lawyer knew you better, he would be your friend. It is the Judge's job to sit there impassively and watch. They know what's going on.

168. All children love to ride on the shoulders of their parents. It is truly the top of the world.

169. I had to hear the stupidest, most unthinking, most hurtful and self-damning thing I ever said in my entire life played, live in court in my own words, in my own voice, eight times.

170. Marriages don't last. When I meet a guy, the first question I ask myself is, "Is this the man I want my children to spend their weekends with?" Rita Rudner

171. Information is power.

172. If you become aware that there are shortages of supplies for the child in the other household, offer to fill some of these needs for the other parent. Do this in a manner that will allow the other side to accept. A gesture of help, offered in a negative manner, indicates that you intend to discredit the other parent, rather than help the child.

173. For your child, build bridges over problems to the other parent, not walls.

174. An adult's personality is built of memories from childhood.

175. If everybody thought before they spoke, the silence would be deafening. Gerald Barzan

176. Do not allow yourself to be drawn into petty arguments.

177. Make sure that, if you have control of the child's report cards, school notes, special awards and results of medical exams, you send copies to the other parent as quickly as possible.

178. Just because two people argue, it does not mean they do not love each other, and, just because they do not argue, it does not mean they do.

179. Consider your child's emotional health and well-being. Think of how your child feels when things are said or done. Learn what is important to your child and make an effort to understand things from the child's point of view. Speak on your child's level and listen to what the child is trying to express, rather than just the words.

180. Sometimes when I'm angry, I have the right to be angry; but that doesn't give me the right to be cruel.

181. You shouldn't be so eager to find out a secret. It could change your life forever.

182. Don't waste time when you are with your child, enjoy.

183. The guard at the door of the courthouse asked, "Hi again, are you coming or going?" I answered, "I never left."

184. Follow court orders and mutual agreements regarding visitation and child support to the letter.

185. If you change the conditions of your life, you have changed little or nothing. If you change yourself, you have changed your whole life.

186. No matter how bad your heart is broken, the world doesn't stop for your grief.

187. Life is problems. Living is solving problems. Raymond E. Feist

188. New ideas have a difficult time getting into a person's head and decisions if they have to squeeze between the biases.

189. Do not trust anyone who, when left alone in your room, turns over your papers.

190. Do something new and constructive for yourself. Start walking a mile in the morning before you get ready for work. Learn to make stained glass at the community center. Take an evening class for automotive repair at the junior college, etc.

191. Parenthood: an incident, an occupation, or a career.

192. One of the great disadvantages of rushing to judgment is that the consequences last such a long time.

193. Sciencia es potentia: Knowledge is power.

194. Great love and great achievements involve great risk.

195. Make happy little things important. February is Frozen Potato Month. Make a special day or month for something and celebrate together each year.

196. Communicate with the other parent openly, honestly, and regularly to avoid misunderstandings that are harmful to the children.

197. Make a celebration of making a peanut butter and jelly sandwich with your children.

198. Perjury is not prosecuted in Family Court!
Perjury is not prosecuted in Family Court!
Perjury is not prosecuted in Family Court!

199. When your children say they are sick, make sure it is real. Playing sick can be a good way to get out of doing things they do not want to do or going places they do not want to go.

200. Everything is so dangerous that nothing is really frightening. Gertrude Stein

201. People believe what is whispered before they believe what is shouted.

202. Treat your children with respect and require that they treat you with respect.

203. You can lose friends but enemies accumulate.

204. Confidence is what you feel before you truly understand the problem.

205. Those who live by the sword are shot by those who don't.

206. Never throw mud. You may miss your mark, but you will have dirty hands. Joseph Parker

207. Be reliable, especially for you.

208. Children need substantial contact with the same-gender parent during adolescence.

209. Even if severing the relationship with the other parent is your idea, you will still have to go through the healing process.

210. If you do not learn from your mistakes, you loose twice.

211. When situations arise where immediate action is necessary, take a second look at the whole situation before reacting impulsively.

212. Make plans. If time with your child is limited, make the most of it with several activity options that can be adjusted according to how the child feels, your financial limitations and weather conditions. Visit family and friends, indoor physical fitness centers, or plan a day of activities around your home. Have a "plan A", "plan B" and "plan C.," If everything falls apart, be prepared to handle the disappointment with grace.
213. It is no disgrace to rest a bit. Gene Fowler
214. Power without planning is useless.
215. Both parents have the right to inspect and receive the children's medical and dental records, and the right to consult with any treating physician, dentist, or mental health professional on behalf of the children.
216. A parent's heart is a child's schoolroom.
217. Send your children letters and notes written on different colors, sizes, textures of paper.
218. Worry should drive us to action, not to depression.
219. The liar's punishment is that he cannot believe anyone else. George Bernard Shaw
220. Simplify, and offer solutions.
221. Be an instrument of peace and calmness for your children when they feel fear and anxiety.
222. The main block to transformation is the thought that we shouldn't be where we are, that we should already be further along in our growth than we perceive ourselves to be. Where you are right now is perfect for you; remember, it's just a stop along the journey, and you'll be moving along again soon.
223. Life is a series of new beginnings!
224. If we perspire more in times of peace, we will bleed less in times of war. Chiang Kai Chek
225. You never quite leave your children at home, even when you do not bring them along.

226. Who you were and who you will be are insignificant compared to who you are.

227. Allow all grandparents to continue to have contact with the children.

228. Give your children twice as much of your time and half as much of your money.

229. React realistically by reducing the priorities of unlikely events.

230. PRENATAL: when your life was still somewhat your own.

231. Excessive competitiveness, anxiety, hostility, suspiciousness, all originate in the nursery years. That is why, if we want a world of peace and not violence, love and not hate, cooperation and not murder, justice and not selfishness, we have to learn how to make childhood more happy. No nobler task could be pursued by our generation. Joshua Loth Liebman 1907 - 1948

232. Separate wishful thinking from reality, set realistic goals, and act to bring those goals into existence.

233. Have you ever imagined a world with no hypothetical situations?

234. How you do anything, is how you do everything.

235. We are all prisoners at one time or another in our lives, prisoners to ourselves or to the expectations of those around us. It is a burden that all people endure, that all people despise, and that few people ever learn to escape. R. A. Salvatore

236. We do not see things as they are. We see them as we are. Talmud

237. The only person we can compare ourselves with is the person we were and the person we want to become.

238. I think I can. I think I can. I think I can.

239. A narrow mind and a wide mouth often go together.

240. When people share their feelings with you, strive to understand their point of view.

241. Happiness is not getting what you want, but enjoying what you have.

242. Your child's name on a special cup, and t-shirts from you, to have at their other home, gives you a constant presence. Personalized school notebooks and pencils will also remind the child that you were thinking of him or her.

243. You really are strong enough to handle this, use this opportunity to grow as an individual.

244. Man walked on the moon, but his soul remains riveted to earth. Once upon a time, it was the opposite. Elie Wiesel

245. Make a do not do list. Ask your children what they enjoyed least about the last family outing or visitation. Then try to skip those things next time.

246. Keep promises, both good and bad. If you promise a reward, make sure you give it to your children. If you promise a punishment, make sure that they get it.

247. It's hard to make a comeback when you haven't been anywhere.

248. Take life as it comes. Run when you have to; fight when you must, rest when you can. Robert Jordan

249. Despite all my rage, I am still just a rat in a cage! Smashing Pumpkins

250. If you are an inappropriate parent, even the best lawyer, getting the highest fees, cannot work miracles.

251. You shouldn't seek happiness through things that other people have control over. Otherwise, you end up being enslaved to them. Epictetus

252. He who angers you conquers you. Elizabeth Kenny Australian Nurse

253. It is more important to know where you are going than to get there at record speed.

254. Carefully let the child know how you feel about them not living with you, and that he or she remains in your heart.

255. When attempting to gather information, it is important to remember that most people prefer to exchange information rather than give it away. Tell a person something and they will try to top it.

256. Everything you do may be wrong. However, do everything for the right reason.

257. A loving atmosphere in your home is the foundation for your child's life. Especially if a loving atmosphere does not exist in the other home.

258. Assure your child that the problems you and the other parent are having are due to adult behavior and not the child's behavior.

259. Take photos of everything. Include photos of child-oriented projects you and your "significant other" do with your child. Happy events are important to you now, to your case soon, and to your child in the future. It is also necessary to document dirty, unsafe or worrisome conditions to which your child is exposed. On the other hand, when you are accused of something, or fear that you may be, use a photo. Taking a photo with a camera that prints the date on the photo is very good evidence.

260. Seek professional guidance to correct any antisocial or dysfunctional attitudes or behaviors your child may exhibit. Mediators and judges are favorably impressed with parents who are able to put their own embarrassment aside to make sure their child receives positive help to heal emotional problems. This assures that the child will function more efficiently as an adult.

261. The trouble with being in the rat race is that even if you win, you are still a rat. Lily Tomlin

262. Generally speaking, others are acting in exactly the same manner that you would under exactly the same circumstances.

263. My wife got the house, the car, the bank account, and if I marry again and have children, she gets them too. Woody Allen

264. Make a to do list. Most children do not know what to do to help get things ready for a trip or a party. Tasks might include: Gather up everyone's pillows for the trip. Sweep the front sidewalk. Empty all the little wastebaskets in each room into the big one that goes out to the trash.

265. Worry does not empty tomorrow of its problems. It empties today of its joy.

266. Some act first, think afterward, and then repent forever. C. Simmons

267. Include your child as a member of the family with the chance to give and receive affection, express anger, and learn how to manage these feelings in himself and in other members of the family.

268. Have the courage to make necessary changes.

269. Having seen you do so much with so little for so long, your children begin to expect you to do everything they want with nothing from them.

270. Depression is merely anger without enthusiasm.

271. It is lack of discipline when I do something other than acts or deeds that will further me in the direction that I say I want to go.

272. When you do anything, keep the 3-r's in mind:
Respect for self
Respect for others
Responsibility

273. There is no need to judge where you are in your journey; right now, it's enough that you are traveling.

274. Be what you want them to see.

275. Take good care of the pets, gardens and things that are important and must be left behind by your child when he has to be away from your home. Your child is suffering many losses of which you are not aware. Each loss compounds the great sadness your child feels. Do your best to safeguard those things your child need not lose.

276. It only takes one person to change your life. You.

277. Goals, unlike wishes, are specific results achievable only by a realistic plan.

278. Your words and thoughts bend your reality.

279. Do not get in the habit of weeping with your whole heart without learning to laugh with your whole heart.

280. Make an effort to fill your life with people who love you and treat you well. This will give you the strength to fight when necessary.

281. Not getting what you want is sometimes a wonderful stroke of luck.

282. Sometimes, the people on your team have to tell you things you do not want to hear.

283. It is frightening to learn of the temptations our children face. Remind your children there are alternatives, and provide them with the sources and resources to make positive choices.

284. In every divorce case, the other side consists of the rapists, murderers, child molesters, adulterers, embezzlers and liars. Why did you have children with such bad people in the first place?

285. Move beyond ego.

286. You may be disappointed if you fail, but you are doomed if you do not try. Beverly Sills

287. If we wait for the moment when everything, absolutely everything is ready, we shall never begin. Ivan Turgenev

288. On commercial airlines, they tell parents to always put on their own oxygen mask first, and then take care of their children. You cannot help a child if you pass out in the process. You have to be okay before you can help your children.

289. Tough times do not last. Tough people do.

290. Protect your child from seeing or being drawn into parental disputes or disagreements.

291. Silence is sometimes the best answer.

292. Warning: Dates on the calendar are closer than they appear.

293. What happens around us is largely outside our control, but how we choose to react is inside our control.

294. Assure your child of both parents' love.

295. Time is a very special gift of God; so precious that it is only given to us moment by moment.

296. You do not plan to fail. You fail to plan.

297. If you act with your child's welfare in your heart, you do not have to work so hard in your head to fix things.

298. Your children learn about your honesty and integrity by the examples of what they see you do, not by what you say you do.

299. Let the child know that you are very happy that he or she can be with you. Do it often.

300. If something is broken when the child is with you, fix it and send it home with the child in good order. It reduces the aggravation with the other parent and shows your child that you care about what is important to the child.

301. If you cannot do it out of love and a real willingness, do not do it.

302. Some people seem to know more when you try to tell them something than when you ask them something.

303. Perfection is not necessary; there is no arriving, only going.

304. Proof of the truth is out there. What are you doing here?!

305. Give compliments freely and sincerely.

306. Custody Battle: the longest guilt trip you'll ever take.

307. If someone is a jerk to you, don't be a jerk back. They always catch the second person.

308. When you send letters and notes to your children, keep them upbeat and include a piece of chewing gum, some jokes or a dollar bill.

309. Success: To laugh often and love much, to win the respect of intelligent persons and the affection of children; to earn the adoration of honest critics and endure the betrayal of false friends: to appreciate beauty; to find the best in others; to give one's self; to leave the world a bit better, whether by a healthy child, a garden patch or a redeemed social condition; to have played and laughed with enthusiasm and sung with exultation; to know even one life has breathed easier because you have lived--This is to have succeeded. Ralph Waldo Emerson

310. Read the Sunday funny papers and comic books together.

311. Anyone can produce children. However, it takes someone special to be a parent.

312. We do not have to stand back and let others determine if we are to be happy, sad, fearful, or loved.

313. Rehearse your lines. The other parent isn't going to change from the last time you had to deal with him or her. Have nice answers ready for any of the usual hurtful or just plain stupid things that might be said.

314. Be the change you want to see in the world. Mahatma Gandhi

315. When you lose, do not lose the lesson.

316. I complained that I see my child only once a week, until I met some parents that had not seen their children in years.

317. When you lie, your children know it. When you lie to your children, they never forget.

318. Handle discussions or disagreements with the other parent over the telephone or privately, out of sight and hearing of the child. This will decrease the amount of stress felt by the child at times of pick up or delivery or when both parents are able to attend an event with the child.

319. Everybody is somebody else's weirdo. Dilbert

320. Every person, all the events of your life are there because you have drawn them there. What you choose to do with them is entirely up to you.

321. Do you see difficulties in every opportunity or opportunity in every difficulty?

322. You must be consciously aware of pulling your thoughts back from the past to the present moment in order to maximize your energy to create a positive, forward-looking present.

323. Real love for your children always creates, it never destroys, especially someone or something your children love.

324. I just had to let it go. John Lennon

325. One must think like a hero to behave like a merely decent human being. May Sarton

326. Observe the situation as a spectator not a participant.

327. The measure of your ignorance is the depth of your belief that anything bad that happens to you is an injustice and tragedy. What the caterpillar calls the end of the world, the Master calls the butterfly.

328. Decide to be happy. Your children need that.

329. After a day in court, you may need to take a drive. You will like the feeling of getting your hands on something you can control.

330. If you have a church home and have been thinking about attending church on a regular basis, this is a good time to renew those bonds. If you have not established religious ties, consider doing so now. Most mediators and judges attend church.

331. Perhaps ... someday ... our ability to love won't be so limited. Gates McFadden as Beverly Crusher "Star Trek: The Next Generation"

332. As children succeed, the family thrives.

333. Catastrophic events will happen in the lives of your children. They watch how you deal with these events now to know how to deal with their own later.

334. Watch for unusual behavior your child may exhibit when dealing with a specific person, place or circumstance. Aggressive or drastically subdued behavior may indicate unspoken fears your child may have or a need for specific attention.

335. Martin Luther King, Jr. said that faith is taking the first step, even when you don't see the whole staircase.

336. Key to being an emotionally healthy child is to have parents who have the ability to respect their child's differences and not perceive them as betrayals.

337. When you must do something and it makes you feel uncomfortable, look at the reasons for your apprehension and ways to overcome them.

338. Alone again, naturally.

339. Try to spend as much time with your child as you can. If court orders or distance limit the time you can spend with the child, stay in touch other ways. Send letters, post cards and call (at reasonable hours) if you cannot make a physical appearance. Keep promises to your child.

340. Recognize in your child's life the really important moments. Help your child see them and enjoy them. Soon it will be too late.

341. Life is taking chances - chances are changes.

342. Renew your membership or get involved with family oriented groups and organizations such as church, boys' and girls' clubs, Campfire Girls, Boy and Girl Scouts, and PTA.

343. If it is a mistake of the head and not the heart do not worry about it, that is the way we learn. Earl Warren

344. There are no rules of success that work unless you do.

345. Doubt is the beginning of learning.

346. You will not be respected unless your are respectable.

347. Enroll your child in a summer program, an after-school or weekend youth development program in which you can volunteer your time and participate. Most of these groups are starved for parental assistance. Volunteer at your child's school.

348. The world will never look the same.

349. It is just as important to know what you will stand for, as it is to know what you will not stand for.

350. Comfort your child in times of stress and let your child comfort you. Practice some reassuring answers to your child's concerns.

351. Educate yourself as to the legal and emotional issues involved in the process of custody.

352. It takes more strength deciding what to do than doing it.

353. You cannot argue with an idiot, without looking like an idiot!

354. When your small child is tugging at your clothes, kneel down, look your child in the eye, smile and listen.

355. Turbulence is life force. It is opportunity.

356. Maintain proper supplies for the child's needs in your home. Seasonal clothing (cool enough for summer as well as warm enough for winter), vitamins, foodstuffs generally identified for the age of the child (as well as anything especially suggested for this youngster) with ongoing input from the child's doctor.

357. Evaluate the purpose of your actions and tasks today to be sure they are relevant to your goals.

358. You do have rights, but justice is not automatic.

359. You may be a better parent for a teenager than you are for a toddler. Don't expect to be the perfect parent for all stages of your child's growth and development. Do the best you can with what you have and who you are. Most of all, be patient and kind to your child and to yourself.

360. Live for today, yesterday was hard enough.

361. Do not correct your children's mistakes in front of other people. Tell them how to improve when nobody is around.

362. Do not keep changing your mind about what you want your children to do. Make up your mind and stick to it.

363. As you decide to make positive changes in your life that will affect custody, make sure your actions are sustainable.

364. Solve problems with your children. Do not overwhelm them with catastrophic dilemmas, but let them help you work things out. Example of a problem the child cannot handle: "Where are we going to find $372.00 to pay two months of telephone bills?" Example of a problem a child can understand and help with: "How do we get started faster in the mornings so we will not be late for school and work? How about, if we put the breakfast bowls and spoons on the table the night before? Can you think of anything else we can do?"

365. Do try to make peace with the other parent. Try again, and again. Start new each time. It is worth it for the child.

366. We could never learn to be brave and patient if there were only joy in the world. Helen Keller

367. Whatever hits the fan will not be evenly distributed.

368. Get the children a subscription to a magazine that would be of interest to them. Then every month when it arrives the children will be reminded that you thought of them.

369. It is reasonable to be dissatisfied with the results of your efforts without being discouraged.

370. Promptly notify the other parent if you are unable to make a scheduled appointment with your children.

371. If you are lucky enough to get to, hug your child.

372. Both parents' have a right to be notified in case of the children's serious illness.

373. When your children do something wrong, do not try to get them to tell you why they did it. Sometimes, they do not know why themselves.

374. If I were to choose between pain and nothing, I would choose pain, again and again. W. Faulkner

375. The human brain starts working the moment you are born and never stops until you begin to speak to the other parent.

376. Expect trouble as an inevitable part of life and repeat to yourself, the most comforting words of all; This too, shall pass. Ann Landers

377. The best thing for sadness is to learn something. T.H. White

378. If you are the parent lucky enough to live with the children, take time out and get excited to see the papers they bring home from school each day.

379. Everyone has already made all the allowances they are going to make for the personal misfortunes of your life. Do not talk about them anymore. Move on.

380. Make your home a predictable environment. Keep schedules and routines (with reasonable flexibility) on which your child can count. When temporary or permanent change is necessary, explain these at the child's level of understanding, with calm assurances as to why and when the change will happen. This is especially important for your child if the other home is in constant flux.

381. My children do not come from a broken home. We fixed it. We got a divorce.

382. Help the child understand that, although he or she may have done something incorrectly or wrong, the child is still a good person.

383. If you are blessed with the ability of persuasion, use your skills to help your children for their own self-improvement, not to your advantage.

384. Love and respect are the most important aspects of parenting, and of all relationships. Jodie Foster

385. If you want a place in the sun, you have got to put up with a few blisters. Abigail Van Buren (Dear Abby)

386. Keep the lines of communication open between you and the other parent.

387. Make sure all child support or spousal maintenance is current in this or any other matter before you enter this custody battle. Any back money owed will give you "dirty hands in the eyes of the court". Children are very hurt that a parent does not care enough about them to send money for their care.

388. Do what you can, with what you have, where you are. Theodore Roosevelt

389. Separate your children from their unacceptable actions. You love your children, but may not like what they are doing at a given moment. Help your children understand the difference.

390. When it gets dark enough, you can see the stars. Lee Salk

391. It is hard to fight an enemy who has outposts in your head. Sally Kempton

392. To be absolutely certain about something, one must know everything or nothing about it. Olin Miller

393. Not everything that can be counted counts, and not everything that counts can be counted. Albert Einstein

394. Here is my checkbook, car keys, and credit cards. I am officially resigning from adulthood. If you want to discuss this further, you will have to catch me first, cause, Tag! You're it.

395. Channel your negative compulsive thoughts into constructive energy and activities.

396. Children who feel insecure will exhibit regressive behavior.

397. Keep all receipts. Mark purchases made specifically for the child and total separately on the receipt. Try to pay for products and services for the child with a separate check, listing the check number on the receipt. Do not attribute all general purchases to the child. Keep receipts of purchases for the child in a separate box or file.

398. Talking about arranging visitation, support or other obligations that concern the parents with the children is forcing children into the conflict and is bad parenting.

399. Be honest with your child. It is easier for your child to understand that you have made mistakes and are embarrassed about something, than it is to know that his parent is a liar.

400. When you come to a roadblock, take a detour. M. K. Ash

401. Unless you choose to do great things with it, it makes no difference how much you are rewarded, or how much power you have. Oprah Winfrey

402. Life is offering you many opportunities; have the courage to experience them.

403. Do not fight, argue with, or degrade the other parent in the presence of your children.

404. It is human nature to think wisely and act foolishly. Anatole France

405. When you are very angry or upset, walk around the block, counting each step as you take it, and concentrating on your pace and the length of stride. This will rest your angry emotions and give the dangerous part of your feelings a chance to cool off.

406. You may use your mind to learn from the past and plan for the future, or to bitch about the past and worry about the future.

407. Balance avoidance, acceptance, and surrender.

408. Everybody needs a place to rest; Everybody wants to have a home; Don't make no difference what nobody says; Ain't nobody wants to be alone. Bruce Springsteen

409. Both parents should have the right to authorize emergency medical, surgical, hospital, dental, institutional, and/or psychiatric care.

410. It does not require many words to speak the truth. Chief Joseph (Nez Perce)

411. You cannot change the past, but you can ruin a perfectly good present by worrying about the future.

412. What you do not know may not hurt you, but it may amuse the opposition.

413. Be aware that children learn chiefly by the example of their early caregivers and learn quickly by what they see, not by what they are told.

414. Life is not the way it is supposed to be. It is the way it is. The way you cope with it is what makes the difference. Virginia Satir

415. Just when in the relationship did Snow White turn into the Wicked Witch of the West?

416. Keep yourself and your child in a safe, non-threatening environment.

417. If it were not for STRESS, you would have been out of energy long ago.

418. When you become angry with your children, resist the temptation to recite a list of their faults and failings. Instead, explain your frustrations, listen to theirs, and together work on a plan to use in the future.

419. Do not answer verbal assaults.

420. Engage your child in conversation. Listen to what your child says.

421. Get someone else to blow your horn, the sound will carry twice as far and the tone will ring more clear.

422. One often learns more from ten days of agony than from ten years of contentment. Merle Shain

423. Live simply, expect little; forget yourself and think of your children. This is the recipe for happiness.

424. Know what is more than enough.

425. Make plans directly with the other parent rather than through the children.

426. Maybe if I call my child custody battle a hobby, I will not mind the expense so much.

427. I exist, I am, I am here, I am becoming; I make my life and no one else makes it for me.

428. May some of the kindness and joy you have given away return to you the day you need it most.

429. Each obstacle or problem you face is a challenge. Make sure each challenge brings out the best in you. You will be judged by how you responded to the challenge not how many or which challenges you faced.

430. Do not agree to any type of 50/50 arrangement unless it appears that you can work well together and that the children can flourish in such an environment.

431. One-half of knowing what you want is knowing what you must give up before you get it. Sidney Howard

432. Little of what might happen does happen. Salvador Dali

433. Often people can see farther through a tear than through a telescope. Leo J. Muir

434. There are risks and costs to a program of action; but, they are far less than the long-range risks and costs of comfortable inaction. John F. Kennedy

435. Foster hope, health, and happiness in others and in yourself.

436. Remain constantly prepared to be surprised. Face the unpleasant surprise bravely and enjoy the pleasant ones to the fullest.

437. There are only seven or eight human stories, and they keep repeating themselves as fiercely as if they had never happened before.

438. Avoid self-defeating behaviors and dangerous people.

439. You will teach your children what you are by what you do.

440. You can be just as happy or miserable as you decide to be. Ben Dichter

441. My attorney charged me $20,000 per file box in the office that had my name on it, and adjusted it twice in 3 years for inflation.

442. Talk to your children about what is important in their lives such as soccer games, piano recitals, report cards and their best friends.

443. Do not give in. Do not give up.

444. Having children, even a houseful does not make you a great parent any more than owning a car makes you a winning racecar driver.

445. Subscribe to the newspaper. If you cannot afford daily delivery, get a subscription for Sunday only, or make it a point to pick up the Sunday edition. The public library has newspapers you may read at no cost. The list of events and activities will give you some good ideas of things to do with your children.

446. Plan and prepare for each phase as if it was "The Big One."

447. We know the game is fixed. But if you do not play you can't win.

448. When you start with revenge, you have already lost.

449. If you do not believe them and get happy when they say good things, why do you believe them and get upset when they say bad things?

450. Get rid of the drama. Everyone is tired of the excuses and stories. Show them you are willing and able to handle your life, yourself, and your children.

451. Categorize and resolve.

452. Send your children pictures of yourself doing current activities. Include newspapers articles, cartoons, odd facts, today is..., poems.

453. Who will you be today?

454. The Sheathed Sword: To fight and conquer in all your battles is not supreme excellence. Supreme excellence consists of breaking the enemy's resistance without fighting. In war, then, let your object be great victory, not lengthy campaigns. True excellence is to plan secretly, to move surreptitiously, to foil the enemy's intentions, and balk his schemes, so that at last the day may be won without shedding a drop of blood. Sun Tsu

455. The law is all that remains when we have forgotten all we have been taught.

456. You may be right, I may be crazy. But it just may be a lunatic you're looking for. Billy Joel

457. Face and conquer any fears about yourself as a person and a parent.

458. Life is a patchwork - here and there are scraps of pleasure and despair joined together by hit or miss.

459. Well it's all right now; I've learned my lesson well; You know you can't please everyone, so you've got to please yourself. Ricky Nelson "Garden Party"

460. Handle problems and learn from all the results you get. If what you are accomplishing with what you are learning is not good for you and your child, change it.

461. Use techniques, such as networking, in divorce and parent support groups. Gravitate towards the positive long-term goal orientated people that attend the meetings.

462. Stay upbeat and positive. Find the lesson in each defeat. Successful generals and coaches study the failed and successful engagement plans of their friends, foes and predecessors. Learn from everyone's mistakes and find solutions to problems.

463. The only cross you bear is the one you choose to carry.

464. God grant me the Senility to forget the people I never liked anyway, the good fortune to run into the ones that I do, and the eyesight to tell the difference.

465. False charges can be dismissed, found against or defaulted, but never erased.

466. UNIVERSAL Rx: No moving parts, no batteries, No monthly payments and no fees; Inflation-proof, non-taxable; In fact it is quite relaxing; It cannot be stolen, will not pollute; One size fits all, do not dilute. It uses little energy; but yields results enormously. Relieves your tension and your stress; Invigorates your happiness; Combats depression, makes you beam; And elevates your self-esteem! Your circulation it corrects; Without unpleasant side effects. It is, I think, the perfect drug; May I prescribe, my friends,... the hug! (And of course, fully returnable!) Henry Matthew Ward

467. Appreciate the value of fresh starts.

468. Attorney: I object to that as being a question impossible to answer; outside this person's expertise; and I don't know what it means.

469. Ask yourself, "What's the best way to marshal the necessary resources?"

470. Let people talk long enough and they will confess everything about themselves with what they say and what they do not say.

471. Give your children the confidence and courage to confront problems early, before they become overwhelming. In addition, remind them they are never alone.

472. All growth is painful. Max Brand

473. Men imagine that thought can be kept secret, but it can not. It rapidly crystallizes into habit, and habit solidifies into circumstance. James Allen

474. We are confronted with insurmountable opportunities. Pogo

475. Much that I sought, I could not find. Much that I found, I could not keep. Much that I kept, I could not free. Much that I freed, returned to me. Lord Byron

476. The joys of parents are secret, and so are their grief and fears: they cannot utter the one, nor will they not utter the other. Francis Bacon

477. Write special letters to each child on his or her birthday. Include a review to the whole year so that each child has a record of what happened each year.

478. What you are speaks so loudly that I cannot hear what you say. Ralph Waldo Emerson

479. Do not separate your children from each other if possible.

480. You can be right or you can be happy.

481. The elementary principle of all deception is to attract the enemy's attention to what you wish him to see, and to distract his attention from what you do not wish him to see. General Archibald Wavell

482. Sometimes you do not get a turn.

483. If you must voice your disagreement with another person, make sure one of these things will happen because of the conversation. There will be an improvement in the lives of children. There will be no escalation of hostility between parents. There will be a new place from which to communicate. Then proceed without making impossible statements, clouding issues and confusing points.

484. There are two souls in my chest, and one is determined to beat down the other. Yes, we do the damndest things to ourselves.

485. Yea, so you are the one on the hot seat, so what?

486. Try to take criticism seriously, but not personally. Hillary Clinton

487. But life without growth is also painful. Pain has a message; learn-adapt-mature. In that sense pain is a helper, a prod. After you see that, you are glad for the experiences that nudge you to advance. Lynella Grant

488. The passage of time gives one the ability to be glad for the helper.

489. Most anger is situational. If the same words were spoken by a different person we would ignore the comment.

490. Question: Do you recall discussing with your attorney, that if you were in a deposition or anything like that and you did not want to give the answer they want, all you have to say is, "I do not know", or "I do not recall"? Answer: No. I do not remember.

491. Millions of people are deaf, but many more will not listen.

492. Endure unkind words without seeking revenge. Be proud of yourself for not succumbing to petty arguing and retaliation.

493. If you choose not to decide, you still have made a choice. Rush from the song 'Free Will'

494. Always give your best, never get discouraged, never be petty; always remember, others may hate you, but those who hate you don't win unless you hate them, and then you destroy yourself. Richard Milhous Nixon

495. Family court has made more liars out of people than the 1099 Tax Form.

496. The small victories in court feel like the joyful slide down a snowy hill. However, with court and sleds the drag back up takes so much longer.

497. Work is of two kinds; first, altering the position of matter at or near the earth's surface relative to the other matter; second, telling other people to do so. Bertrand Russell

498. Some parents miss what is going on because they are broadcasting when they should be tuning in.

499. If you keep doing what you've always done, you will keep on getting what you've always got.

500. Warm hearts and cool heads maintain a comfortable temperature in the mediation room.

501. ...whatever is true, whatever is noble, whatever is right, whatever is pure, whatever is lovely, whatever is admirable-if anything is excellent or praiseworthy-think about such things. Philippians 4:8 (NIV)

502. Communicate in clear, non-judgmental ways.

503. Attorneys are paid to learn from the mistakes they make for others. Find an attorney that does not make those mistakes twice.

504. I apologize for any mistakes I have made, including any mistakes you feel I have made including mistakes of which I was unaware. I sincerely pledge to do my very best, especially in my relations with you and our children. Nobody's perfect; we all make mistakes; yet we can all improve. Above all, I promise to be the best possible parent to our children that I can be, so help me God.

505. We underestimate our power to change ourselves and overestimate our power to change others.

506. If you cannot be a good example, then you will just have to be a horrible warning. Catherine Aird (Thank you. We need both.)

507. The custody battle is a war of boomerangs. Our thoughts, deeds and words return to us eventually, with astounding accuracy.

508. Surprise them. Sometimes say, Yes.

509. Attempt to keep the same set of rules in both homes as much as is reasonably possible.

510. The demand for psychotherapy keeps pace with the supply, and at times one has the uneasy feeling that the supply may be creating the demand ... Psychotherapy is the only form of treatment which, at least to some extent, appears to create the illness it treats. Jerome Frank

511. You are right. It is not fair. Feel better?

512. It is not who is stronger. It is who is strong longer.

513. In the appropriate circumstances, rightly placed silence is perceived as confidence, and confidence is believed to be born of strength.

514. We do not deal much in facts when we are contemplating ourselves. Mark Twain

515. Sometimes 1 + 1 makes 11.

516. Anxiety is a matter of choice. What is or is not going on around us does not determine whether events are stressful. Anxiety is an inability to step back and examine the real penalties or damage that may occur or even if the perceived threat is valid or manufactured.

517. Try? There is no try. There is only do or not do. Yoda, the Jedi Warrior

518. There is no blame for failing to achieve any goal, only for failing to make the effort and to use whatever talents and resources available to you.

519. Do everything in your power to protect your rights. However, always weigh your rights against your child's well being.

520. Help older children remember the things that are important to the other parent and grandparents, such as birthdays, mother's, father's and grandparent's day. The child will appreciate your assistance in pleasing someone for whom the child cares. It also shows the child that he or she can be somewhat neutral in this custody battle and is free to give and receive love from both sides. Your unselfish and reasonable behavior will be appreciated by your child.

521. Over-stressed body or mind will not serve you well.

522. The only good advice I ever got for free was "Never eat at a cafe called Mom's. Never play cards with a man named Doc. Never lay down with a person that has more problems than you have."

523. Watch for and take advantage of opportunities. Do not fill your hands with them and then let them slip through your fingers like sand until they are gone.

524. It is more important to do right than to be right.

525. Stay involved in your children's lives, doing the best you can to make their lives as special as you can and at the same time maintain some balance in your own life.

526. The identity relationship between parent and child is direct, demonstrable, and basic. Remember they are as ephemeral as you are and as susceptible to chance destruction.

527. What you choose to see in the people and events going on around you alters what occurs even before you decide if you will make any response at all.

528. There is no scarcity of opportunity; there is only a scarcity of resolve to make it happen.

529. Your efforts will be judged by their results.

530. Every gun that is made, every warship launched, every rocket fired signifies, in the final sense, a theft from those who hunger and are not fed, those who are cold and are not clothed. This world in arms is not spending money alone. It is spending the sweat of its laborers, the genius of its scientists, and the hopes of its children... This is not a way of life at all in any true sense. President, General, D.W. Eisenhower

531. When you fail to admit and accept your responsibility for all of your experiences, and blame others, you are giving away your freedom to change yourself and control your life.

532. Do not get prepared. - Stay Prepared.

533. If you lose the use of your right hand, it is terrible. But, the quality of your life is up to you, not your hand. Do not let your dead hand rule your life.

534. The difference between intelligence and stupidity is that intelligence has its limits.

535. Your children are the living message you send into the future.

536. The difference between a together person and a crazy person lies in the way they put their angry feelings in perspective. Richard Carlson

537. The difference between a terrorist and the court is that you can negotiate with the terrorist!

538. Life is much like a card game. You have no choice in the cards dealt to you, but how you play. Those cards can mean the difference between winning and losing.

539. The difference between perseverance and obstinacy is, that one often comes from a strong will, and the other from a strong won't. Henry Ward Beecher

540. Pain is an event; suffering is a process. Understanding the difference between pain and suffering gives us a chance to handle the suffering part differently. Much of our suffering is the result of the voices of conditioning we all carry around. Listen to what those voices say without believing them or acting upon them. Your life will be different.

541. The difference between fiction and reality? Fiction has to make sense. Tom Clancy

542. If you are not following Your Plan, you are most assuredly following Someone Else's.

543. Sometimes, when we do not get what we want, we realize that what we got is what we would have wanted had we known what we would have gotten in the first place.

544. Never trust anyone who thinks you should rely on them instead of yourself.

545. Do not consider making changes when you are tired, hungry or frightened.

546. Your children love you: win or lose.

547. I remember being where you are. Some days you are not sure you will survive. Some days you are not sure you want to. However, you do, and there will be many days you will be glad you did.

548. Good judgment comes from experience, and often experience comes from bad judgment. Rita Mae Brown

549. A good attorney can understand those who cannot explain ideas clearly, and can explain to those who are not very good at understanding.

550. Said the five year old to the guardian ad litem, "You listen to me nice. I sure wish you liked me good enough to be my parent."

551. Treat the other parents as if they were what they ought to be and you help them to become what they are capable of being, and what your children need.

552. Deal with problems patiently.

553. And the wind said: May you be as strong as the oak, yet flexible as the birch; may you stand tall as the redwood, live gracefully as the willow; and may you always bear fruit all your days on this earth. Native American prayer

554. Children are unpredictable. You never know what inconsistency they're going to catch you in next. Henry Ward Beecher

555. To be happy is easy enough if we give ourselves, forgive others, and live with thanksgiving. Joseph Newton

556. When you feel held back by, impatient with, or are too tired to deal with your children, imagine the grief of not seeing them again.

557. We will either find a way, or make one. Hannibal

558. The thoughts you have each hour of each day are building your life. You are creating your destiny.

559. A family is more than a group of people who have keys to the same house.

560. You do not have to knock yourself out planning grand, special activities involving your children. Simple times together will do.

561. Usually you have the answer. Sometimes you just have not asked the right question.

562. Your children do not remember years, they remember moments.

563. The grand essential to your child's happiness in this life is to do something with you. Share love and have something for which to hope.

564. Even in the darkest phase; Be it thick or thin; Always someone marches brave; Here beneath my skin" K.D. Lang

565. Accept the "help" your children give. Not everything needs to be done "right". If you can, simply say, "You made the bed. Good for you.", and leave the bed as the child made it even if it is not perfect.

566. When someone does not understand you, do not get upset. Attempt to understand the message that person received that you did not mean to send.

567. Your children will come to realize, when it happens, that you did not decide when and how to die; but they will realize that you did decide how you would live.

568. If things go wrong today, do not blow up, bounce back.

569. There is no better way of exercising the imagination than the study of law. No poet ever interpreted nature as freely as a lawyer interprets the truth. Jean Giraudoux

570. Accept simple solutions.

571. There is the letter of the law. There is the spirit of the law. This means do not use the letter of the law to be mean spirited.

572. Fear limits our choices. Refuse to choose when you feel the cold teeth of fear on your neck.

573. The truth for each individual is not cold and permanent. Each person defines what they think to be true filtered through personal experience and need. Then as they attempt to live with those truths, they discover they may not serve well. A new truth is then identified and accepted.

574. Events are never random. They always have a pattern and a discernible timing. Learning to read and correspond to the patterns will increase your power.

575. Your strategy should not be etched in stone, just almost.

576. Give yourself permission to find some laughter, joy, and fun in each day.

577. Let the children know, "We all love you and want you to have nice things and nice experiences in both families."

578. The art of being wise is the art of knowing what to overlook. William James

579. Final court dates really brighten a home. The closer they are, the later the lights are on.

580. It's hard when you discover what keeps you going, keeps you all alone. Blue Rodeo

581. Experience is what you get when you did not get what you wanted. It is also when you get what you said you wanted, but not what you meant you wanted.

582. Once you have risen to the occasion under pressure, stay there. Many things will be clearer to you from up there.

583. Stupidity is the inability to learn from mistakes. Rossonavich

584. Your living is determined not so much by what life brings you as by the attitude you bring to life. Not so much by what happens to you as by the way your mind looks at what happens.

585. Make these "the good old days" for your children.

586. Your children's feelings are more important to you than you being right or proving the other parent wrong.

587. The crisis of yesterday is the joke of tomorrow. H.G. Wells

588. Other people's reactions to your victories are sometimes different than you expect. Try to understand their reactions and accept their feelings.

589. Keep your goal fixed very clearly in your mind.

590. Respond responsibly, especially to inappropriate behavior and situations.

591. Not everything is perfect - You cannot expect that.

592. We must use time creatively, and forever realize that the time is always ripe to do right. Nelson Mandela

593. If you stop to think, do not forget to get started again.

594. Life is too short to spend it collecting grievances, losing one's temper, writing people off, seeking the easy way out, running in circles, keeping score, satisfying negative urges, wasting time, leveling criticism, pitying oneself, sending dirty looks, reliving regrets, planning revenge, avoiding responsibility, and laying blame.

595. On any journey, you must find out where you are before you can plan the first step.

596. You deserve to be happy regardless of your marital or custodial status.

597. Avoid rabidly biased witnesses. Even your own.

598. Use generous and flexible discretion as to the time and frequency of calls to the children.

599. When you are uncertain, reject feelings of self-pity. Look at your good qualities and accept them as gifts to use graciously.

600. One waits in vain for psychologists to state the limits of their knowledge. Noam Chomsky

601. You can never get enough of what you really do not need to make you happy.

602. A horse you cannot ride is better off gone.

603. When you establish rules in your home, make certain every family member understands them. Then enforce them fairly, because not doing so causes confusion and distrust.

604. Be calm, in front of coworkers, family, friends, or your children.

605. Set down on paper stories of your children's personal events including pets, travels, friends, hobbies, interests, new learning and ordinary happenings. Read them to your children when you get to be with them. Read them to your children over the phone if you don't get to see them. Save the stories for your children. There will be a day you can share the stories with them.

606. Indecision is torture.

607. If you know the other parent cannot accept help from you for any reason, find ways to help without telling them where the help came from.

608. Help and encourage the children to remember the other parent on special occasions, allowing the children to telephone on a reasonable basis.

609. In the Jewish belief a mitzvah is a good deed that one does at the highest level, or those that are done anonymously. Performing a good deed for your children must be an even higher blessing. Sending money to the utility company, phone company, or childcare center are good examples.

610. Concentrate on the qualities you find most desirable in others and discover them within you.

611. Put a ban on grumbling and complaining in your home for your children and yourself. This will assure a more positive environment.

612. A good plan violently executed right now, is far better than a perfect plan executed next week. General George Patton

613. Consider your children's emotional health and well-being. Think of how they feel when things are said or done between you and the other parent. Children are part of both parents and if you hate something about the other parent, then you must hate some part of the child.

614. Be an appropriate role model for the children

615. Concentrate on all the things you have, not all the things you do not have.

616. Resolve to be tender with the children, patient with the know-it-all's, sympathetic with those in pain, and tolerant with the weak and the wrong. Sometime in your life, you will have been all of these.

617. Do something nice for someone with more problems than you.

618. Let the children see where the other parent is going to live after he or she moves out of the house.

619. Instead of automatically saying no, try to say yes first.

620. Both parents have the right and responsibility to consult with school officials concerning the children's welfare and educational status, and to inspect and receive student records, if law allows.

621. When I left home and faced the realities of the world, I put my thoughts of God in cold storage for awhile; because, I could not reconcile what I believed, deep inside, with what was going on around me. But that early period, when God was as real as the wind that blew from the sea through the pine trees in the garden; left me with inner peace, which, as I grew older, swelled – until, perforce, I had to open my mind to God again. Jane Goodall

622. Sit together to read. Even if your are each reading (or looking at) a different book.

623. Teach your children to analyze their errors and learn from mistakes. Then give them another chance to improve their performance.

624. You cannot do everything at once; you can do something at once.

625. Do not foster the children's feelings of guilt over the custody process.

626. When you are frustrated over your limitations, when there are things you want to do, but cannot; if your limitation is time, may you find the way, if your limitation is knowledge, may you learn the way.

627. Keep your eyes, ears and mind open so you can distinguish and seize opportunities.

628. Control yourself. You cannot make a scene

629. Once you see the effects or symptoms of a problem, look for the underlying causes. Ask, “What is really going on here?”

630. There are some second chances.

631. If you ever get to sit on the porch with your higher power, take the opportunity to say thanks to God for lending you your children.

632. If it is a bad day, do not add up all the unpleasantness. That may be all you see now, but not all that is there. You have probably been through a day just like this or much worse and survived it, or made it into a good day.

633. Show children how things are done. Then let them do it. Maybe they can write the check, change a spark plug, or copy a file to a floppy disk.

634. It is difficult to argue a point when the opponent is unencumbered with an understanding of the facts.

635. Do not communicate with the other parent through the children.

636. Put aside differences with the other parent long enough to attend school conferences together.

637. It is important to remember that tomorrow the sun will rise, people will go to work, babies will be born and life will go on.

638. There are two freedoms; the false, where people are free to do what they like; the true, where people are free to do what they ought. Charles Kingsley

639. The upward paths may be the hardest, but they have the best views. Neil Peart

640. Parents should live as close to each other as is practical, convenient, and reasonable.

641. Psychological traps like self-blame or blaming the other parent are like cement blocks on your legs. You have to free yourself from the old emotional battles. Many things just are.

642. Evaluate and adjust your expenditures for better results.

643. If the other side, or the attorney for the other side, uses tactics that are upsetting, don't give them the satisfaction of letting it upset you.

644. When a child does something incorrectly, show the child several ways to accomplish the same task.

645. Extra love from you goes into a child's psychological bank account, which draws interest and can be used for an emotionally rainy day.

646. May the road rise to meet you. May the wind always be at your back. May the sun shine warm upon your face, the rains fall soft upon your fields, and, until we meet again, may God hold you in the palm of his hand. Irish Blessing

647. A great parent is one who offers a child another view of reality without making the child wrong.

648. Let the child know that you are very happy he or she can be with you. Do it often.

649. A hero does what an ordinary man does; he just does it for five minutes longer. We can be heroes, if just for one day. David Bowie

650. The custody of your children is only one aspect of the care they need.

651. Call the people who care about you each week. Make a list of things to ask them about. How is your mother doing? Is Kelly finished with that special class at school? Did that new club improve your game? Make an effort to focus on their lives. It will give you a break from your worries.

652. A problem becomes a problem if we allow it to be a problem.

653. You cannot do a kindness too soon, for you never know how soon it will be too late. Ralph Waldo Emerson

654. Let your children know you have a photo of them in your wallet and or appointment book.

655. If it hurts your feelings, but not hurt your child, let it go.

656. Remember where you came from, where you are going and why you created the mess, you got yourself into in the first place.

657. If you want to be loved, do not criticize those you want to love you.

658. I asked God to grant me patience. God said "No. Patience is a by-product of tribulations; it isn't granted, it is earned."

659. A good person can do something bad and a bad person can do something good.

660. If family court is a game, for many of us the object is to find out the object of the game.

661. Maintain normal household routines as much as possible.

662. Every holiday is an opportunity to send your child a card. Even if the child lives in your home full time. Children get very little mail addressed to them and enjoy the experience.

663. Trust yourself, no matter what.

664. Failure is like riding a bicycle. You do not fall off unless you stop peddling.

665. Speak when you are angry, and you will make the best speech you will ever regret. Lawrence J. Peter

666. As you begin to evaluate each situation in terms of whether it is important to the happiness and well-being of your child instead of whether it imposes on you or not, this will all get easier for you.

667. You are stronger than your worries and fears. The worst possible thing that can happen usually is not what happens anyway. The worries and fears that lurk in the murky depths, below the surface, just out of sight gnawing, groaning and causing the sense of unease that steals your sleep in the dark of night can be tamed. Their power depends on them staying unclear and having the opportunity to keep cutting back in the line of concerns several times; thereby, multiplying their weight. Put a pad and pen next to the bed and list the subterranean monsters by capturing them on the paper so you can deal with them in the light of day.

668. The strategy you use depends on your goals for your case and how you define "win."

669. If you do not know where you are going, you will probably end up someplace you do not want to go.

670. Make the least of the worst and the most of the best.

671. You can complain because roses have thorns, or you can rejoice because thorns have roses. Ziggy

672. The most valuable gift a parent can give a child is a good example.

673. Your children are like sponges. They absorb all your strength and leave you limp. Give them a squeeze, and you get it all back.

674. If it does not affect the welfare of your children, let unkind words or deeds go unanswered.

675. You can believe in someone and still doubt what they say.

676. Make cookies together.

677. Watch your children carefully as they interact with other children. The stories they play out may give you an insight into how the world appears to them.

678. Make an effort to be kind, caring, considerate, receptive, patient, and aware.

679. Communication skills include knowing when not to talk.

680. To be someone you are not is not only schizophrenic, it is very energy draining.

681. The important things are always simple. The simple things are always hard.

682. The last of the human freedoms is to choose one's attitudes. Victor Frankl

683. Those who do not know how to weep with their whole heart do not know how to laugh either. Golda Meir

684. Have your recent actions been furthering you in the direction you want to go?

685. Bloom where you are planted.

686. Do not allow the children to act out too much in response to the divorce process.

687. The way I see it, if you want the rainbow, you gotta be willing to put up with the rain. Dolly Parton

688. Children are never detached spectators when their parents fight. Learn to restrain yourself to protect your children.

689. You are never given a wish without also being given the power to make it come true. However, you may have to work at it.

690. Do not miss the invaluable opportunity to hold your tongue.

691. A War Chest must include a sharp mind, a strong spirit, a stout heart and money.

692. Let your children know that they belong with both parents in both homes and that you want them to feel good about being happy in each environment. Include each child as a member of the family with the chance to give and receive affection, express anger, and learn how to manage these feelings in themselves and from other members of the family.

693. I used to have a handle on life, but it broke.

694. Do not be unduly impressed and influenced by attorneys and judges.

695. All the flowers of tomorrow are the seeds of today!

696. The Special Garden you can plant with your children that will feed them for the rest of their lives. First, plant five rows of peas: Preparedness, Promptness, Preservation, Politeness, and Prayer. Next, plant three rows of squash: Squash Gossip, Squash Criticism, and Squash Indifference. Then five rows of lettuce: Let us be faithful, Let us be unselfish, Let us be loyal, Let us be truthful, Let us love one another. And no garden is complete without turnips: Turn up for church, Turn up with a smile, Turn up with determination.

697. A child is the root of the heart. Carolina Maria de Jesus

698. A Creed For Those Who Have Suffered
I asked God for strength, that I might achieve.
I was made weak, that I might learn humbly to obey.
I asked for health, that I might do great things.
I was given infirmity, that I might do better things.
I asked for riches, that I might be happy.
I was given poverty, that I might be wise.
I asked for power, that I might have the praise of men.
I was given weakness, that I might feel the need of God.
I asked for all things, that I might enjoy life.
I was given life, that I might enjoy all things...
I got nothing I asked for -- but everything I hoped for.
Almost despite myself, my unspoken prayers were answered.
I am, among men, most richly blessed! Roy Campanella

699. If you teach your children how to make helping others a priority, they will learn that the world does not revolve around their own problems.

700. The art of life is to know how to enjoy a little and to endure much. William Hazlitt

701. You need to press on, but you must remember it is OK to take time to rest. You can accomplish so much more if you are refreshed and renewed.

702. Ambition is when your dreams put on work clothes.

703. The true and noble way to kill a foe, Is not to kill him, -- you, with kindness, may so change him, that he shall cease to be so. And then he's slain. Alain

704. Family law has become so complicated and therefore expensive, that it takes a lot of money to even get beaten.

705. Many of life's failures are people who did not realize how close they were to success when they gave up. T. Edison

706. If our American way of life fails the child, it fails us all. Pearl S. Buck

707. Trying, is usually an excuse for not doing.

708. Every person thinks God is on his or her side.

709. A benefit of being in the parents' rights group for a long time, is you can make new mistakes while advising others who are making old ones.

710. Not every day, but today, I get to see the ones I love today!

711. Of course everything has been said that needs to be said. But since you were not ready to hear it yet, it has to be said again.

712. Don't let life discourage you; everyone who got where he is had to be where he was. R.L. Evans

713. The more preparation you do, the luckier you get.

714. When someone disagrees with you, do not decide it is a reason to argue. View it as an opportunity to see another point of view. It may be a chance for you to become aware of new elements, emphasis and strengthen your understanding of why you are right or let you see the error in your thinking.

715. A Day... is a miniature eternity. Ralph Waldo Emerson

716. If all our misfortunes were laid in one common heap from which everyone must take an equal portion, most people would be contented to take their own and depart. Socrates

717. It is common for parents to have hundreds of photos of just their children or the children with the other parent during happier times, playing with neighbor children or pets. What they do not have are any of themselves with their children. Make an effort to have photos of you and your children taken.

718. Life can only be understood backwards, but must be lived forwards. Soren Kierkegaard

719. Be a good listener. Your ears will never get you in trouble. Frank Tyger

720. Decide to solve the problem. Decide to tell the truth. Decide not to interrupt. Decide not to call names.

721. Watch for unusual behavior your child may exhibit when dealing with a specific person, place, or circumstance. Aggressive or drastically subdued behavior may indicate unspoken fears your child may have or a need for specific attention.

722. Any child can have a clean room. All that is needed is patience, organization, and a full time maid.

723. Bedtime is a prime example of test time in the real world. When you are surrounded by unhappy children in several stages of disrepair, ingeniously inventing doomsday scenarios to prolong the evening, remember you are here because you love them.

724. Begin to live as you wish to live.

725. We have forty million reasons for failure, but not a single excuse.

726. Rationalization is a mental technique which allows one to lie or cheat without feeling guilty.

727. Guard your thoughts. They may become words at any moment.

728. Some parents believe it is their job to talk, and the child's job to listen. Unfortunately, the child often finish before the parent.

729. Integrate what you believe in every single area of your life. Take your heart to work and ask the most and best of everybody else, too.

730. We think in generalities, but we live in detail. Alfred North Whitehead

731. Teachers open the door, but you must enter by yourself. Chinese Proverb

732. Remember, the children are always watching.

733. What the world needs is some "do-give-a-damn" pills. William Menninger

734. Let the children know that even though they may not live with you, they remain in your mind and heart. Children need to know that just because they are out of your sight they are not out of your thoughts.

735. It is as hard to see one's self, as to look backwards, without turning around. Thoreau

736. How many cares one loses when one decides not to be something, but to be someone. Coco Chanel

737. Many candles can be kindled from one candle without diminishing it. The Midrash

738. If you know the enemy and know yourself, you need not fear the result of 100 battles. If you know yourself, but not the enemy, for every victory gained, you will also suffer defeat. If you know neither the enemy or yourself, you will succumb in every battle. Sun Tsu

739. The opposition's attorney was professionally trained to infuriate and destroy.

740. We make a living by what we get. But we make a life by what we give. Winston Churchill

741. We can only teach what we most need to know.

742. Avoid exhibiting the obnoxious smirk of a tough kid on high ground when you win an argument or point in court.

743. Kneel down if necessary, and look your children in the eyes when you talk to them as often as you can.

744. The best way to become boring is to say everything. Voltaire

745. A barking dog is often more useful than a sleeping lion. Washington Irving

746. Every exit is an entrance somewhere else. Tom Stoppard

747. Advice to witness in court: Be sincere, be brief, be silent.

748. Your lie will surface at the worst possible time for you, cause the most damage to your case, and afford you the least amount of opportunity to make amends.

749. Not everyone has to take sides.

750. Learn from the times your efforts with the other parent failed. Do not repeat behavior that will initiate a negative response. Do it better each time and without malice. Try to make things work. Do not keep track of the times your efforts failed, only of the times your efforts let everyone win.

751. Information will give you confidence. Confidence will give you control. Control will give you perspective. Perspective will give you strength. Strength will give you power. Power will give you the WIN.

752. Start new family traditions to celebrate with your children. Plant a tree each year at the end of winter. Put together some pads for dogs and donate them to the animal shelter. Build a birdhouse to celebrate summer vacation. Fix some broken toys and donate them for homeless children.

753. The critics do not count, or the people who count you out, nor the people who point out where you stumbled, or where you could have done better. The credit belongs to you, the one in the arena whose face is marred by dust and sweat and blood, who strives valiantly, who errs, and who comes up short again and again, who knows the great enthusiasms, the great devotions, spending yourself in a worthy cause. At best, you know the triumph of high achievement and at worst, if you fail, fail while daring greatly, so that your place will never be with those cold timid souls who never knew victory or defeat.

754. We do not inherit the earth from our ancestors, we borrow it from our children. Haida Indian Saying

755. Photographs are just as important to small children as they are to you. Give toddlers the extra copies or photos that you do not like. They enjoy looking at themselves and it helps them see themselves as a real person.

756. Do not wait to be asked. Deliver proper supplies for your child's needs to the other parent's home and the child's school.

757. It would be a mistake to judge your life by someone else's definition of happiness.

758. Never doubt that a small group of thoughtful, committed citizens can change the world. Indeed, it is the only thing that ever has. Margaret Mead

759. Spend time in your child's School or Sunday School class.

760. Make new family traditions for you and your children in your home. Popcorn an hour before bedtime, candles at dinner time or stargazing on the lawn.

761. Many of life's most valuable lessons can only be learned by failure.

762. People change and forget to tell each other. Lillian Hellman

763. Protect your children. Life has taught us that love does not consist in gazing at each other, but in looking outward together in the same direction. Antoine de Saint-Exupéry Wind, Sand, and Stars

764. Too good to be true, is a tug-of -war between hope and logic.

765. If you feel guilt or others reprimand you for not being a good parent in the past, remind them and yourself, the only way to repair damage from the past is to do better now. Moreover, you are doing better now.

766. It is easier to get forgiveness than it is to get permission.

767. Kindness is the inability to remain at ease in the presence of another person who is ill at ease, the inability to remain comfortable in the presence of another who is uncomfortable, the inability to have peace of mind when one's neighbor is troubled. Rabbi Samuel H. Holdenson

768. Respond to all situations in the most positive mind-set you can. Try again. And again. For your children, try yet again.

769. If you live your life simply by avoiding unpleasantness, every undesirable situation will dictate your behavior.

770. Build a birdhouse with your child. A small project that bonds the child to you and helps a bird.

771. Life is not a matter of milestones, but of moments. Rose Kennedy

772. Comfort your child in times of stress and let your child comfort you. Practice some reassuring answers to your child's concerns. Example, "We have always worked it out before. We can do it again."

773. Do not think dishonestly.

774. Be less critical of your child and yourself.

775. It's the most unhappy people who most fear change. Mignon McLaughlin

776. It is a very short trip. While alive, live. Malcom Forbes

777. If you can find an old diary or journal, you wrote 10 or 20 years ago, read it. It will help you put this time of your life in perspective when you see what was important to you then and how the worries of that day worked themselves out.

778. As you mourn the things you wanted and did not get, remember to celebrate all the things you did not want and did not get.

779. Remember what you are there for once you arrive.

780. If you are providing insurance for your child, make sure the insurance company gives you two cards with the child's name so you and the other parent can have one. This will eliminate any delay in treatment for your child in an emergency. Additionally, young adults should have a card in their wallets.

781. We only see what we are prepared to see.

782. Assure your child of both parents' love.

783. Make the most of every failure. Fall forward.

784. When you are arranging your plans to accommodate the other parent, don't guess. Ask about specific dates and times.

785. When you get your children a subscription to a magazine that would be of interest to each of them have a subscription of the same magazine sent to your home. This will give you some ideas with which to start conversations, and the children and they will have familiar reading material at your home when they visit.

786. The public library is a great place to spend an afternoon with your children.

787. When you come to the edge of all the light you know, and are about to step off into the darkness of the unknown, faith is knowing one of two things will happen: There will be something solid to stand on, or you will be taught how to fly. Barbara J. Winter

788. Share your child's hobby, school successes, and sports achievements.

789. To appreciate the heaven of being with our children, it is good to have some fifteen minutes of hell thinking you will be without them forever.

790. Since there is no way to avoid it, plan for your next meeting with a difficult person. Write down the sequence of events the way they usually happen. Now change the way you would normally have dealt with the situation. List other options you have tried that have had some success and several new options. Review your lists just before you have to see this person. You will feel a new control. Do not be drawn into the old pattern.

791. You grow when you give. Volunteer at your child's school.

792. Learn to accept your child as a person separate from yourself and the other parent. Find ways to demonstrate your acceptance.

793. You are all you will ever have for certain. June Havoc

794. Separate your child from the child's unacceptable actions. You love your child, but may not like what that child is doing at a given moment. Help your child understand the difference.

795. The only place you will find success before work is in the dictionary. May B. Smith

796. Half of the harm that is done in this world is due to people who want to feel important. They do not mean to do harm. They are absorbed in an endless struggle to think well of themselves. T.S. Eliot

797. Discovery, experience, judgment, knowledge, intelligence, wisdom, generosity, character.

798. Never look down on anybody unless you are helping him up. The Reverend Jesse Jackson

799. Life is the ultimate hobby. It meets all the criteria. It is expensive, takes a lot of time, you have to do it yourself, it is fun to share with the people you care about and the more time and effort you spend on it, the better it comes out.

800. When going forth with anger, withhold the sword. When going forth with sword, withhold the anger. Miyamoto Masashi

801. All my life I've wanted to be somebody. But I see now I should have been more specific. Jane Wagner

802. The truth of the matter is that you always know the right thing to do. The hard part is doing it. General H. Norman Schwarzkopf

803. Snowflakes are one of nature's most fragile things, but just look what they can do when they stick together. Vista M. Kelly

804. Be patient and kind to your child and to yourself.

805. There will always be good reasons why you did not do what you said. And they are all distortions of the true reason. It does not matter whether the deed itself is noble or trivial. The harm comes from how you feel about having to do it now that you said you would. Just do it. It takes less energy to do the neglected deed than the inner turmoil that is created by avoiding it. The price we pay for avoidance is our integrity.

806. Life is a process of becoming, a combination of states we have to go through. Where people fail is that they wish to elect a state and remain in it. This is a kind of death. Anais Nin

807. Take your vitamins.

808. Some people are molded by their admirations, others by their hostilities. Elizabeth Bowen

809. If it is working, keep doing it. If it is not working, stop doing it. If you do not know what to do, do not do anything.

810. Anything can happen to you tomorrow, but at least nothing more can happen to you yesterday.

811. Resist victimizing yourself with feelings of guilt. Talk to your children about what is important in their lives, baseball games, piano recitals, report cards and their best friends.

812. A parent goes into a custody battle with fear, with respect, with awareness, and with absolute commitment, aware of the pain, but not indulging in it is the trick.

813. Life is what happens to us while we are making other plans. Thomas La Mance

814. Like everyone else, you are an imperfect and fallible human being, so there is no sense in punishing yourself if you occasionally fall short of what you expected. If things don't go your way, you don't have to blame yourself if you know that you gave it your best effort. Instead, give yourself a reward and take some credit for your good intentions and for having tried so hard.

815. Caution: In the courtroom your “big break” could be your heart.

816. Do not do anything to the other parent that you would be ashamed for your children to see or know about.

817. We choose to make of this life either a palace or a prison.

818. It is the very nature of government to oppose changes and reforms, and mistreat its critic. Henry David Thoreau

819. At the end of each day take time to make a plan for the next day. Example, review what you have scheduled for the next ten days and specifically review the next day or two. Wednesday 6:00am go to the gym to work out, 7:30am go to work, 11:30am lunch with Shawn, 5:00pm exchange books at library, 7:00pm call children, 8:00pm watch the movie, Forrest Gump.

820. I am not so smart that I cannot make foolish choices. I am not so strong that I cannot be broken. I am not so confident that I cannot despair. I am not so aware that I cannot be fooled. I am not so determined that I cannot fail. So what!

821. Road rage, postal rage, telephone rage, airline rage, technology rage and family court rage. Do not be road kill on the highway of life. Be kind to yourself, your children and others.

822. Not all advice is distilled wisdom. It always reflects the values and philosophy of the advice giver. It always relates to a particular time, place and circumstance, and may not work in other settings.

823. Tis the motive that exalts the action; Tis the doing, and not the deed. Margaret Preston

824. Avoid becoming accustom to frequently requesting and/or accepting help in any form, from any one person or source. It is addictive, disabling and ultimately destroys your dignity.

825. No real or imagined discomfort should keep you from improving the relationship you have with your children.

826. You grow up the day you have your first real laugh at yourself. Ethel Barrymore

827. Do not be afraid your life will end; be afraid that it will never begin. Grace Hansen

828. Man's mind that stretched to a new idea never goes back to it's original dimensions. Oliver Wendell Holmes

829. Although everything is possible, nothing is easy.

830. Put your feelings in a diary. It is a sane, healthy way to express and work through your feelings.

831. Character is finishing the task after the passion has left you.

832. Some attorneys work hard at being jerks, some do not have to.

833. When everything is going badly and you are trying to make up your mind, look towards the heights. No complications there. Charles De Gaulle

834. Custody status does not determine what kind of person you are. Without the burden of day-to-day chores that childcare requires, many non-custodial parents can still influence the lives of their children in many positive ways.

835. The story is polished with retelling.

836. The work will wait while you show the child the rainbow. But the rainbow will not wait while you do the work. Patricia Clifford

837. Avoid imaginations of vengeance or reprisal against the other parent. These feelings are dangerous for you and negatively influence your children. Get counseling for guilt or anger.

838. Make every effort to keep bitterness and regret from damaging your relationship with your children.

839. Almost all our faults are more pardonable than the methods used to hide them.

840. Worry less about your rights and privileges and more about your responsibilities and obligations.

841. Keep a calendar in a convenient place for the children. The eye level of a child is usually much lower than an adults. The refrigerator is a good place. Help them mark important dates such as events at school, as well as ones you have planned with the children, family and friends-like birthdays and anniversaries.

842. Distinguish between true gain and loss. Do not be guided by hurt feelings.

843. When I die, bury me at the Toy's R Us so my children will still want to come and see me.

844. We've been trying to get down to the heart of the matter. But, my knees get weak and my teeth start to chatter. I think it is about forgiveness, forgiveness even if you do not bother to love me anymore. Don Henley

845. Make words work for you.

846. History teaches us that people and nations behave wisely when they have exhausted all other alternatives. Abba Eban

847. Never mind what the other parent does or says. That's not your concern now. Your job is to get out of it from your end.

848. The best tool for resolving conflict is for each parent to pose this question to any proposal that they are not pleased with, "Is that what is best for (put the children's names in here)?"

849. If everything has gone against you in the past, work with the future. Time is on your side.

850. Let he who is without sin, cast the first stone. John 8:7

851. Beware of news flash junkies.

852. Provide your children with envelopes with your address and postage already attached, so they can send you letters or school papers they want you to see.

853. Anger is momentary madness, so control your passion or it will control you. Horace

854. The desire to control the life of another person is a work of great labor, its possession, a source of continued fear, its loss, a source of excessive grief.

855. K.I.S.S. Means "Keep It Simple Stupid."

856. Four things to learn in life: To think clearly without hurry or confusion, to love everybody sincerely, to act in everything with the highest motives, children re-invent your world for you. Susan Sarandon

857. The measure of a man's real character is what he would do if he knew he would never be found out. T.B. Macaulay

858. Loose lips sink ships.

859. If you do not learn to keep your private business to yourself, you have just shot yourself in the foot. If you have never had this experience... it hurts like Hell you feel stupid., and, you have positively identified yourself to the world as an idiot.

860. If you can't say something nice, shut up!

861. So few of us really think. What we do is rearrange our prejudices. George Vincent

862. Is the enemy of my enemy, not my friend? No. Is the friend of my enemy not my enemy? Yes.

863. Aphorisms and quotes remind you of and reinforce basic truths.

864. You cannot cause the other side additional distress. So do not. It will backfire on you.

865. Faults are like car headlights. Those of others seem more glaring than our own.

866. You live longer once you realize that any time spent being unhappy is wasted. Ruth E. Renkl

867. All kids are gifted; some just open their packages earlier than others. Michael Carr

868. The costs of a custody case may force you to work more hours. However, you should not work overtime when your children are staying with you. Your children should spend most of their designated time with you, not in childcare or with others.

869. Remember, we all stumble, every one of us. That is why it is a comfort to go hand in hand. Emily Kimbrough

870. When things go wrong, do not go with them.

871. Example is not the main thing in influencing others. It is the only thing. Albert Schweitzer

872. Confidence, like art, never comes from having all the answers. It comes from being open to all the questions. Earl Gray Stevens

873. You cannot engage in questionable activities. Usually, it is best to avoid even the appearance of questionable activities. In order to win, there are some things that you <u>cannot</u> do. If you are considering doing something questionable, but are not sure you should, don't. Consider how you would feel, or what you would do, if such action were taken against you. If what you're considering doing will make the situation worse, it will affect your case negatively. If you are not sure about doing something, ask your attorney, police department, or your private detective. Use common sense.

874. A year from now you may wish you had started today. Karen Lamb

875. You cannot use your children as pawns to ransom things or favors from the other side.

876. Even a fool, when he holdeth his peace, is counted wise; and he that shutteth his lips is esteemed a man of understanding. Proverbs 17:28

877. The will to win is not nearly as important as the will to prepare to win. Bobby Knight, coach, Indiana Hoosiers.

878. You cannot live in fear or hatred for extended periods. These strong emotions will make you and your children physically and psychologically ill.

879. Follow your plan and your dream will become your goal.

880. Sometimes, being pushed to the wall gives you the momentum you need.

881. The time to be happy is now. The place is here.

882. You cannot stop keeping a detailed log just because things seem to be going well. You have dealt with these people and know they will not change. The appearance of normal behavior they are exhibiting after years of unreasonable behavior is a warning not a gift.

883. You cannot use your children to remind the other parent about money or other obligations.

884. Nothing produces such odd results as trying to get even. Franklin P. Jones

885. You cannot do everything in an attempt to please and win back the other side to the kind of relationship you desire.

886. For small children, record bedtime stories. A new one for each week.

887. When the problem is solved, the solution will be obvious.

888. Sometimes it takes years to really grasp what has happened to your life. Wilma Rudolph

889. Peoples' actions depend largely upon the fear that they feel.

890. To handle yourself, use your head; to handle children, use your heart.

891. You cannot spend your time daydreaming about the happy times you had with the other side in the past.

892. Anger is only one letter short of danger.

893. If anger is not restrained, it is frequently more hurtful to us than the injury that provoked it. Seneca

894. Children still need to love and be loved by both their parents.

895. To understand your parents' love you must raise children yourself. Chinese Proverb

896. It is never "OK" to hit or spank a child or commit other acts of violence.

897. If your child has a computer and is, "on-line", communicate through e-mail or chat rooms. It can be less expensive than telephone bills.

898. You cannot yell, cuss out, or berate attorneys, police, judges, court mediators or the other side, no matter how upset you are.

899. Get organized. Little things first.

900. Do not worry about failure. Worry about the chances you miss when you do not even try.

901. I finally figured out the only reason to be alive is to enjoy it. Rita Mae Brown

902. Fill your child's life with experiences, not excuses.

903. My favorite quote is "Life is too short to be little," written by Disraeli. Often we allow ourselves to be upset by small things we should despise and forget. We lose many irreplaceable hours brooding over grievances that, in a year's time, will be forgotten by us and by everybody. No, let us devote our life to worthwhile actions, feelings, to great thoughts, real affections and enduring undertakings. Andre Maurois

904. Realize there is no right time to feel happy or sad. Your feelings are legitimate.

905. Heads are wisest when they are cool. Ralph Bunche

906. You do not just stumble into the future. You create your own future. Roger Smith

907. We must develop and maintain the capacity to forgive. He who is devoid of the power to forgive is devoid of the power to love. There is some good in the worst of us and some evil in the best of us. When we discover this, we are less prone to hate our enemies. Dr. Martin Luther King, Jr.

908. Make the world worthy of your children.

909. Beware of friends applauding inappropriate behavior. They do not understand the risks you are really taking.

910. Protest long enough that you are right, and you will be wrong.

911. We are not interested in the possibilities of defeat. Queen Victoria

912. Be careful what you show – and what you do not show. Marlene Dietrich

913. What poison is to food, self-pity is to life. Oliver C. Wilson

914. Have your child's school send you a schedule of your child's study guide for the year that lets you know what the child will be studying at each part of the year. This will give you an opportunity to offer assistance for school projects.

915. There is a transcendent power in example. We reform others unconsciously when we walk upright. Anne Sophie Swetchine

916. You cannot discuss with the children any problems you may be having with the other parent. There is nothing they can do to improve the situation, and it will cause a great deal of additional stress on them.

917. You cannot worry about winning. It is really about getting what you want and sometimes you lose now to get what you want later.

918. You cannot have anything to do with drugs. You cannot hold drugs for a friend. You cannot package or transport drugs. You cannot buy, sell, or trade drugs. You cannot have anything to do with people involved with drugs.

919. Control your emotions or they will control you. Samurai Maxim

920. You cannot let your children do without necessities. If you are unable to supply seasonal clothing, vitamins, age-appropriate food (with ongoing input from the baby's doctor), it is your responsibility to petition the other parent and/or social service organizations to get what your child needs. Your attorney may assist you in this.

921. Time is a dressmaker specializing in alterations. Faith Baldwin

922. The ability to make people believe in you and trust you is one of the few fundamental qualities of character.

923. You cannot call the other parent at his or her job.

924. You may not cause the other side to lose his or her employment or interfere with his or her ability to earn a living.

925. You cannot violate any court order for any reason.

926. You cannot criticize the other parent in the presence of the children or let others criticize the other parent in the presence of the children.

927. Be where they can find you when they are ready to be with you.

928. When everything the other parent does or says irritates you, make a list of all these things. Then have a meal, get some rest, have another meal and then look at the list you made. Put a 'C' next to the listings that the other parent does because he/she cannot help it. Put a 'H' next to the listings that the other parent does out of habit. Put a 'S' next to the listings that the other parent does out of stupidity. Put a 'G' next to the listings that the other parent does just to get to you. Put an 'A' next to the listings that the other parent does that will actually hurt your children. Now only react or worry about or fix the 'A' List.

929. Fun is a good thing. But only when it spoils nothing better. George Santayana

930. Always do right. This will gratify some and astonish the rest. Mark Twain

931. #1. Totally and completely forgive yourself for the mistakes of the past. #2. Do everything necessary to avoid making the same mistakes.

932. Once false accusations are disproved, they make the accuser appear to be a vindictive pathological liar.

933. You cannot learn parenting skills without either: (A.) A happy growing experience of your own or (B.) Child development or parenting classes. If you have not had one, you will need the other. You cannot let the limits of your own experience, time, or money stop you from getting assistance. Community colleges, parenting classes, clubs, parents' books, and magazines are easily available. Be willing to learn more about being the best parent you can be.

934. You cannot spread gossip about the other parent.

935. Never underestimate the power of words to heal and reconcile relationships. Kind deeds do even more.

936. Excellence is not something you can apply to some things but a habit that improves everything you do.

937. It is too easy to let time take you away from your child, but how wonderful it is to learn the secret of taking time with your child.

938. Parents' priorities change during a custody case. Children's real priorities do not.

939. Fear is a state of mind.

940. You cannot tap or bug the opposition's telephone, even if you supplied the telephone and are paying for the service.

941. You, yourself, as much as anybody in the entire universe deserve your love and affection. The Buddha

942. Nothing in this world can take the place of persistence. Talent will not. Nothing is more common than unsuccessful men with talent. Genius will not. The world is full of educated derelicts. Persistence and determination alone are omnipotent. The slogan, "Press on" has solved and always will solve the problems of the human race. Calvin Coolidge

943. Set realistic goals. Wishes do not always come true.

944. There are no short cuts to any place worth going.

945. Forewarned is forearmed.

946. As far as it depends on you, be at peace with all people.

947. Do not underestimate your importance to your children.

948. If a phone is too costly for you or the other parent to provide, inquire about a digital pager. It would be reasonable for you to call back within an hour of the pager signal. The court considers a willingness to cooperate with the other parent a key issue in deciding custody.

949. If someone tells you; "I wish I could cut your heart out and eat it." Believe them.

950. Never network in a psychiatric ward. Peggy Noonan

951. Learn to really enjoy the accomplishments of others. They will love you for it.

952. You cannot make your children inaccessible to the other parent when the children are in your care. The other parent must have reasonable telephone contact with the children during their normal waking hours. Guidelines for checking on an infant would be 8:00 a.m. to 8:00 p.m. Calls to and from children old enough to talk may reasonably be limited to 10 minutes per child, and would be adjusted according to the age and maturity of the child. If you cannot afford a telephone, ask if the other parent would be willing to bear the cost of a telephone to have easier access to his or her children.

953. You cannot harass, bribe, threaten, or coerce anyone in person or on the telephone. You cannot have another person do these things on your behalf.

954. You cannot refuse proper supplies for the children's needs from the other parent. Make the other parent aware of shortages in a manner that will permit him or her to offer assistance.

955. If you are in a chemical dependency program, you cannot drop out. If you have dropped out, go back and complete the program.

956. Never tell a child, "Now that does not hurt." Always show concern and take the time to kiss and make it better when the child is wounded. As the child gets older you can help them "brush it off" by dusting the area lightly but deliberately, and saying, "brush it off honey."

957. You cannot attempt to sneak information to the court or psychologist.

958. You cannot lie to your attorney. Lying is stupid and will prevent the attorney from doing a good job for you.

959. You cannot blame the other side for all the problems that caused the failure of your relationship.

960. You cannot use aggressive or negative language to refer to or describe the other side. You should not do it in public or in private because it will reinforce a bad habit. It also exposes your children to antisocial terminology that they will invariably repeat at the most inopportune time.

961. When they are after your butt, answer the phone. Senator Alan Simpson

962. You will find more instances of the abridgement of your rights by gradual and silent encroachments of those in power than by violent and sudden usurpations.

963. You have a choice. It may not be a choice you like, but it is still a choice. Michelle Pfieffer as LouAnne Johnson in Dangerous Minds

964. Do not build your entire case on the testimony of one person. The judge may disqualify or refuse to hear the testimony, or the person may not show up for court.

965. A lone shipwreck survivor on an uninhabited island managed to build a crude hut in which he placed all that he had saved from the sinking ship. He prayed to God for deliverance, and anxiously scanned the horizon each day to hail any passing ship. One day, he was horrified to find his hut in flames. All that he had was gone. To the man's limited vision, it was the worst that could happen and he cursed God. Yet the very next day, a ship arrived. "We saw your smoke signal," the captain said. Walter A. Heiby

966. You cannot pump your children for information about the other parent's life-style, friends or anything else.

967. Ignorance of the law is no defense. If you do not know the law ask a professional.

968. You cannot fight with the other side in the presence of your children.

969. There is no absolute failure. Sometimes we just do not get all the results we expected.

970. You cannot refuse to give prompt, responsible information about the children's health, location, or welfare to the other parent.

971. Yesterday is history, tomorrow is a mystery, and today is a gift. That is why they call it the present.

972. If you cannot bend, you will break.

973. You cannot violate international, federal, state, county, city, or the moral laws of the community in which you live. You are the one responsible for finding out if any activities you are considering doing yourself, asking someone else to do, or hiring someone else to do, are against the law. It is your business to know what is legal and what is not.

974. It is easier to forgive an enemy than to forgive a friend. William Blake

975. Get and stay healthy yourself. Get plenty of rest, exercise, nutrition, and support.

976. Two things you cannot get back, words and time.

977. Write it down.

978. Parents begin by making intricate conditional promises to one another, both sides with fingers crossed behind their backs, will not work. Will it?

979. People deal too much with the negative, with what is wrong. Why not try to see positive things, to just touch those things and make them bloom? Thich Nhat Hanh

980. Do not let your fear of pain stand in the way of your children's happiness.

981. You cannot spend the short time you have with your children lamenting about how limited the visit is. Do not wait until the children arrive to decide what to do. Do not agonize over the activities you are unable to provide because of time, money, or personal inability. If you have made plans, but the children arrive with alternate activities that seem important to them, make every attempt to be flexible and fulfill their needs.

982. Good News: The court gave me exactly what I asked for. Bad News: That is not what I meant.

983. Those interested in perpetuating the present conditions are always in tears about the marvelous past that is about to disappear without so much as a smile for the young future.

984. Remain vigilant and keep listening for any deficiencies or trial balloons you see the opposition send up. If something the other side does or says today would have caused you concern when things were at their worst, do not pass it over now. Really examine what has happened. Make the proper people aware, using an incident report, and then proceed carefully.

985. You cannot invade the privacy of the other side's home with electronic video or listening devices.

986. One is taught by experience to put a premium on those few people who can appreciate you for what you are. Gail Godwin

987. Reassure the children that they will be safe, sheltered, and cared for.

988. You cannot disconnect the children from established patterns. If your children live in the other parent's home 50 percent of the time or more, attempt to maintain the same sleeping, eating, and homework routines established there.

989. Tape-record your children's voices, laughing if you can, with your parents' voices if you can.

990. Laugh often and much, to win the respect of intelligent people and the affection of children, to earn the appreciation of honest critics and endure the betrayal of false friends, to appreciate beauty, to find the best in others, to leave the world a bit better, whether by a healthy child, a garden patch, or a redeemed social condition; to know even one life has breathed easier because you have lived. This is to have succeeded! Ralph Waldo Emerson

991. You cannot be emotionally dependent on your children to fulfill your psychological or physical needs, or to take away the hurt others have caused you. You cannot expect your children to make up for all of the love you may have missed.

992. This above all, to thine own self be true. And it must follow as the night the day, thou canst not then be false to any man. William Shakespeare (Hamlet)

993. Do not attempt to handle everything at once. Break problems or projects into bite-size chunks.

994. Some people approach every problem with an open mouth. Al Gore

995. Do not become confused about what you want. Concentrate on what is important. Motivate yourself and your army. Separate what is not really important from what is.

996. Twelve Things To Remember: 1. The value of time. 2. The success of perseverance. 3. The pleasure of working. 4. The dignity of simplicity. 5. The worth of character. 6. The power of kindness. 7. The influence of example. 8. The obligation of duty. 9. The wisdom of economy. 10. The virtue of patience. 11. The improvement of talent. 12. The joy of origination. Marshall Field

997. Do not bring up the other side's problems with sex or drugs if the problems are not current.

998. I keep my ideals, because in spite of everything, I still believe that people are really good at heart. Anne Frank

999. Dream as if you'll live forever. Live as if you'll die today. James Dean

1000. If you learn from your suffering, and really come to understand the lesson you were taught, you might be able to help someone else who's now in the phase you may have just completed. Maybe that's what it's all about after all...

1001. Be sure that your children understand that the breakup was not their fault.

1002. Do not disappoint your children by not showing up when you have made plans or promises.

1003. Peace is not an absence of war; it is a virtue, a state of mind, a disposition for benevolence, confidence, justice. Baruch Spinoza

1004. The important thing is not to stop questioning.

1005. You cannot make your children choose between yourself and the other side.

1006. You cannot let your attorney aggravate this already sensitive situation with inflammatory words when communicating with the other side. If you have hired a "Mad Dog" attorney, this will be a major problem for you all through the case.

1007. Love means to love that which is unlovable; or it is no virtue at all. G.K. Chesterton

1008. You cannot have your children carry messages to the other parent in order to spare yourself a confrontation. The stress this causes in children is very harmful.

1009. The palest ink is better than the best memory.

1010. Encourage the kids to express their feelings about the breakup in safe ways. Drawing, writing, and talking to calm adults are some of those ways.

1011. All men and women are born, live, suffer and die; what distinguishes us one from another is our dreams, whether they be dreams about worldly or unworldly things, and what we do to make them come about... We do not choose to be born. We do not choose our parents. We do not choose our historical epoch, the country of our birth, or the immediate circumstances of our upbringing. We do not, most of us, choose to die; nor do we choose the time and conditions of our death. But within this realm of choicelessness, we do choose how we live. Joseph Epstein

1012. You cannot get arrested for anything. Any arrest will impact negatively on your suitability as a good parent.

1013. Be absolutely determined to enjoy what you do. Gerry Sikorski

1014. Every man dies. Not every man truly lives. Braveheart

1015. We are what we repeatedly do. Excellence, therefore, is not an act but a habit. Aristotle

1016. Keep the parental role. Be an adult, the children will find that reassuring.

1017. It is never too late to give up your prejudices. Henry David Thoreau

1018. When you are experiencing bouts with fatigue and worry, do not let yourself imagine the other side has more power than they really have.

1019. The test of a first-rate intelligence is the ability to hold two opposing bits of information that are true.

1020. I was always looking outside myself for strength and confidence but it comes from within. It was there all the time. Anna Freud

1021. There are two lasting bequests we can give our children: One is roots. The other is wings. Hodding Carter, Jr.

1022. The more I traveled, the more I realized that fear makes strangers of people who should be friends. Shirley MacLaine

1023. You cannot disappoint your children. Do not make plans or promises beyond your abilities to deliver. If you must change plans, communicate at the children's level of understanding as to why this has happened and when the promise or plan can be carried out. If you encounter this problem more than once, examine your abilities and adjust your commitments. Children do not rebound from repeated disappointments. You must build trust.

1024. Do not explain why you cannot. Decide how to make it happen.

1025. You will be victorious if you have not forgotten how to learn.

1026. Do not make any unnecessary changes. Keep as much stability as possible in daily routines and especially in rules, bedtimes, discipline styles, and socializing.

1027. We need 4 hugs a day for survival. We need 8 hugs a day for maintenance. We need 12 hugs a day for growth. Virginia Satir

1028. You cannot leave angry messages on their answering machine.

1029. I realized that if what we call human nature can be changed, then absolutely anything is possible. From that moment my life changed. Shirley MacLaine

1030. You are no loser. The losers dropped out long ago.

1031. Make a list of things you really want to do with your children and start doing them. One of the symptoms of an approaching nervous breakdown is the belief that the outcome of every action is terribly important.

1032. I was taught that the way of progress is neither swift nor easy. Marie Curie

1033. The moment the emotion self-pity strikes, do something nice for someone with bigger problems than you have.

1034. You cannot criticize your children. It does not help or make them do better. It never changes anything and it breaks their spirit.

1035. Tell the children that they are loved and wanted.

1036. You cannot change the system by fighting it during your case. Work within the current standards and procedures. Learn about what is going on, take names and dates and go after the problems later.

1037. Life is about not knowing, having to change, taking the moment and making the best of it, without knowing what's going to happen next. Delicious ambiguity. Gilda Radner

1038. Start by doing what is necessary; then do what is possible; and suddenly you are doing the impossible. St. Francis of Assisi

1039. You cannot do anything illegal.

1040. Lord, grant me the serenity to accept the things I cannot change, the courage to change the things I can, and the wisdom to know the difference. Reinhold Niebuhr

1041. Working through hardship is an experience that will influence you all the rest of your life.

1042. Do not talk badly about the other parent, their lifestyle or their new partner. Children deserve to be free of the parents' fights; they have a tough enough job already.

1043. Do not lead children to believe in, hope for, or work for a reconciliation that isn't likely to happen.

1044. Every decision involves some risk.

1045. If you are bound and determined to do things wrong, technological progress has merely provided you with a more efficient means of going backwards.

1046. Your good reputation is your most valuable asset.

1047. Scientists support Darwin's claim of more than a century ago. That facial expression could actually intensify emotions. People could really be happier if they forced themselves to smile. Smiling accelerates the manufacture of the chemical hormone serotonin a "natural narcotic" that brings on heightened feelings of well-being.

1048. People are like stained-glass windows. They sparkle and shine when the sun is out, but when the darkness sets in; their true beauty is revealed only if there is a light from within. Elizabeth Kübler-Ross

1049. You cannot attach tracking devices to their vehicles.

1050. Know that your children are fine and doing all the same activities they always have and that you will see them again.

1051. Show your children how much you love them by treating all the people they love with respect.

1052. To live is so startling it leaves little time for anything else. Emily Dickinson

1053. You have to sniff out joy; keep your nose to the joy-trail. Buffy Sainte-Marie

1054. Reasons an attorney will not take your case:
Has already been contacted by the other parent,
Feels you are not being entirely honest,
Feels you will not follow the attorney's advice,
Feels you are not communicating (listening & talking),
Feels you are behaving in an inappropriate manner,
Feels your expectations are not reasonable or flexible,
Feels your case is without merit,
Feels you perceive everything is an emergency,
Feels you cannot afford the legal fees,
Just has too much work already,
Feels your and the attorney's style are not compatible,
Just lost a case like yours and is not willing to try again,
Does not wish to take a case that has already begun, a case from which you have already fired other attorneys, or a case from which other attorneys have already withdrawn.

1055. Tell the people who care about you, what you are going through and how you feel.

1056. Question: "What if the other parent is doing <u>everything</u> wrong?" Answer: "It does not matter." It is none of your business. But you can ask me again when you are not doing <u>anything</u> wrong.

1057. We do not see things as they are, we see them as we are. Anais Nin

1058. The sound of a kiss is not so loud as that of a cannon, but its echo lasts a great deal longer. Oliver Wendell Holmes

1059. Never allow your attorney to stipulate to any agreement you have not read, make sure you understand, and are willing and able to comply with any agreement.

1060. A week is a long time in a child custody battle. But the child's lifetime is the average time spent in a custody battle.

1061. "Beware of anxiety. Next to sin, there is nothing that so troubles the mind, strains the heart, distresses the soul, and confuses the judgment." W. Ullathorne

1062. Do not threaten children with abandonment.

1063. Use this chart to determine what kind of an emergency you are experiencing and who you should call.

Emergency	=	Call
Legal	=	Attorney
Spiritual	=	Rabbi, Pastor, Priest
Medical	=	Doctor, Hospital
Emotional	=	Psychologist or Counselor
Civil	=	Police
Need to Talk or Scream	=	Crisis Line, Hot Line, or Friend

1064. Recognize personal stress symptoms: fatigue, irritability, isolation, sudden mood swings, and major changes in sleeping, eating, and sexual patterns.

1065. If you ask the wrong question, you will always get the wrong answer.

1066. You do yourself more harm in anger than good.

1067. Pain is inevitable. Suffering is optional.

1068. Do not ask your children to be your best friend, sounding board, therapist or confidant. Those roles are for friends and professionals.

1069. If someone makes you angry, upset, hateful, fearful or anything else you do not want to feel they are controlling you, and you are letting them. Take charge of your attitude. Decide how you will face people and situations before you have to do it.

1070. Prepare for the unpleasant.

1071. FROM NOW ON Whenever you have contact with the other parent, with or without others observing, always:

- Act and speak as if you are being taped. *You might be*.
- Listen to the other side and do not interrupt to defend yourself from what is being said or make your point.
- Allow yourself to feel happiness, joy, success and love. You deserve the feelings.
- Accept your feelings. They are not right or wrong; they are just how you feel.
- You know how the other parent feels about you and what the other parent will say.
- Have reasonable non-aggressive responses ready.
- Be clear about why you are dealing with the other parent and what you want to accomplish.
- Practice what you want to say with someone you trust.
- Put your thoughts into proper non-inflammatory language.
- If the other parent interrupts your statement, wait patiently while the other parent speaks.
- Do not get angry or respond to the indictment.
- If you answer the accusations, you are giving the other parent control of the agenda.
- Remain aware of your body language, keeping it open and confident without seeming cold and aloof.
- Be aware of how much time you have to accomplish this task. If there has been a problem in the past, let the other parent know you have five more minutes you can spend here, or that you can be reached by telephone after a certain time.
- Once the other parent has finished, resume your activity or statement.
- Each time the other parent interrupts, wait patiently again.
- Always thank the other parent or anyone else for their time.

- Keep the atmosphere clear. If the opposition “acts up” remember, you are not responsible for or required to respond, you are only responsible for what you do or say.

1072. I fear all I have done is awakened a sleeping giant and filled him with a terrible resolve. Admiral Yamamoto after the bombing of Pearl Harbor

1073. Do not be an immovable object. Be an irresistible force.

1074. Education is what you get from reading the fine print. Experience is what you get from not reading it.

1075. So, when did Prince Charming turn into Ivan the Terrible?

1076. The love of a parent is measured by the sacrifices he is willing to make for the good of his children. If you want to make God laugh, tell him what you are doing tomorrow.

1077. Be yourself --- who else is better qualified? Frank J. Giblin

1078. You can get more with silent infringement than attack.

1079. The ability to take advice is superior to the ability to give it.

1080. Do not ignore the possibility that you may not get what you want in this custody war.

1081. Time is too slow for those who wait and grieve, and too swift for those who rejoice and love.

1082. As a parent, you are never really alone in your thoughts. You are always connected to your child and all who touch your lives.

1083. Go to a support meeting of parents who have lost their children to death. Then re-ask yourself if what you have is so bad.

1084. I object to violence; because when it appears to do good, the good is only temporary; the evil it does is permanent. Gandhi

1085. Things will be better tomorrow.

1086. 1. Timing. 2. Timing. 3. Timing.

1087. Your Attorney Cannot:

- Punish the other side for all that has happened to you.
- Protect you from the truth.
- Get everything you want.
- Win custody for you if you are not a good parent.
- Change the attitude of the court or the laws.
- Handle matters beyond the scope of your agreement.

1088. I remember leaving the hospital, thinking, “Wait, they are going to let us just walk out of here with this baby? We do not know beans about babies! I do not have a license to do this. We’re just amateurs.” A. Tyler

1089. If you have other children, attend to their nurturing and make appropriate arrangements for them when you are not up to daily parenting. They may feel abandoned, jealous, and less loved.

1090. Since you will feel gutted by the custody process it is important to know that the human body can still function quite normally with: all the reproductive organs, one lung, one kidney, the entire stomach, spleen, 75% of the liver, and 80% of the intestines removed.

1091. Weeks may pass where you feel more accepting of your loss of custody, just to be replaced by several viciously angry days. These bad days will also pass. The roller coaster of highs and lows can last several years. Take care of yourself even when you do not feel like it.

1092. It is possible to have opposing ideas in the mind at the same time and still retain the ability to function. One should, for example, be able to see that things are hopeless and yet be determined to make them otherwise. F. Scott Fitzgerald

1093. Do not communicate with the other parent through the children. They aren't couriers or spies, they are children. Send your messages through your lawyers or friends, if you cannot talk to each other.

1094. It is not what you know. It is what you do with what you know.

1095. It is your right and responsibility to stay involved with the children's day to day life including school, after school activities, doctor, counselors, day care providers, etc. If they try to disallow your participation you must take the proper steps to help them understand you are still a parent.

1096. Statistically - 100% of the shots you do not take, do not go in. Wayne Gretzsky

1097. If you are pained by external things, it is not they that disturb you, but your own judgment of them. And it is in your power to wipe out that judgment now. Marcus Aurelius

1098. Limit conversations about your problems.

1099. Keep extra keys hidden some place on your car and outside your home. You know why.

1100. Kindness and intelligence does not always deliver us from the pitfalls and traps. There is no way to take the danger out of human relationships.

1101. Just do it. NIKE

1102. The game is scheduled. We have to play it. We might as well win! Bill Russell

1103. Dr. Robert J. Oppenheimer, supervised the creation of the first atomic bomb. A congressional committee asked, "Is there any defense against the weapon?" "Certainly", replied Dr. Oppenheimer "And that is?" they inquired. Dr. Oppenheimer leaned toward the hushed, expectant audience and subtly whispered, "Peace."

1104. Do not cause hurt... Accidentally or on purpose.

1105. Do not talk, listen.

1106. Carry postage stamps in your wallet or purse. You never know when you will find the perfect card to send to your child or someone who gives you a great deal of support.

1107. Fear defined: false events appearing real.

1108. The walks and talks we have with our two year old in red boots have a great deal to do with the values they will cherish as adults. Edith F. Hunter

1109. Whose Custody Case Is This Anyway?! The court is very sensitive to a case that looks driven or controlled by someone other than the parents of the children. If your husband, wife, father, mother, or significant other gives the appearance of power or passion, you should insist they stay out of the limelight as much as possible.

1110. Nothing can stop the person with the right mental attitude from achieving a goal. Nothing on earth can help the person with the wrong mental attitude. Thomas Jefferson

1111. Find out what conclusions the child has come to about each incident. Set the child straight if the observations are not correct.

1112. A parent always has to think twice, once for the parent and once for the child.

1113. Assure your child you will keep them safe, even if you are not sure you can.

1114. Our children are not going to be just 'our children'. They are going to be other people's husbands and wives, and the parents of our grandchildren. Mary S. Calderone

1115. Make an effort to be sensitive to situations that are happy, sad, or violent. Let your child see that an adult feels and copes in a responsible manner with adult feelings.

1116. It isn't that they can't see the solution. It is that they can't see the problem. G.K. Chesterton

1117. Worry is a misuse of the imagination. It is assuming responsibility that God never intended you to have. It brings sorrow and saps the day of its strength. Alfred A. Montapert

1118. Happiness is based on relationships with people you love and respect.

1119. If it is easy, you are doing it wrong.

1120. Begin difficult things while they are easy. Do great things when they are small. The difficult things of the world must once have been easy; The great things must once have been small... A thousand mile journey begins with one step. Tao-Tse

1121. Nothing is as strong in human beings as the craving to believe in something that is obviously wrong. Joel Achenbach

1122. Yes. There is another option. Find it.

1123. In criminal court, you see the worst people on their best behavior. In family court you, see the best people on their worst behavior. Restated by Janice Palmer Attorney, Arizona

1124. What is done to children, they will do to society. Karl Menninger

1125. By the time a man realizes that maybe his father was right, he usually has a son who thinks he's wrong. Charles Wadsworth

1126. There is an opportunity in all that we do. It is how we use the tools of that opportunity that makes the difference. If you are married or have a significant other, stay as close as possible to this person. The emotional distress you both feel will make communication more difficult. Be patient with each other.

1127. The emotional warfare of the child custody battle is the ultimate opportunity to victimize or protect our children and ourselves.

1128. Don't break your promises.

1129. Circumstances do not make a person, they reveal him or her. Richard Carlson

1130. To be wronged is nothing unless you continue to remember it. Confucius

1131. Some people make things happen, some watch while things happen, and some wonder, What Happened?

1132. Goals that are not written down are just wishes.

1133. Making out the child support check will be stressful every month. Find the easiest way to handle this obligation. Some options are automatic wage deduction or auto-pay through your bank.

1134. You will go from joy to fear like a speeding car thrown into reverse. Set up safety nets.

1135. Other people are not *against* you; they are merely *for* themselves.

1136. Anticipate pangs of sadness on the children's birthdays, holidays and special family times that they cannot be with you. Arrange to celebrate these special days when the children are with you. It is not important that the celebration is not on the "exact" day.

1137. It is not all lies. It could be just Conflicting Truths. It is possible for two truths to appear to be opposite information.

1138. Every expert and professional will tell you, "Above all, do not lie."

1139. There now, you see, it takes all the running you can do to stay in the same place. Louis Caroll

1140. No man chooses evil because it is evil; he only mistakes it for happiness. Mary Wollstonecraft

1141. It is very easy to forgive others their mistakes; it takes more grit and gumption to forgive them for having witnessed yours.

1142. Your love for your child must exceed your need for your child.

1143. If you did not like what the other side did, think about what you would have done, if you were them.

1144. The family court system has: The compassion of the IRS; efficiency of the Postal Service; success rate of the Welfare Programs; enforcement tactics of the Bureau of Alcohol, Tobacco & Firearms, and <u>all</u> at Pentagon prices.

1145. Explain to your child that it is normal to have strong positive and negative feelings.

1146. Talk to your child about any incident that may arise. Ask your child what the child has seen and how the child feels about it.

1147. Keep a diary and one day it'll keep you. Mae West

1148. Who takes the child by the hand, takes the parent by the heart.

1149. The very powerful and the very stupid have one thing in common. Instead of altering their views to fit the facts, they alter the facts to fit their views. This can be very uncomfortable if you happen to be one of the facts that needs altering. Dr. Who

1150. Do not interrupt your enemies when they are making a mistake. Napoleon

1151. A SNAKE IS A SNAKE IS... Snake handlers get snakebite more often than people who avoid the reptiles altogether. Best advice is to stay away from snakes altogether.

1152. Family court is not an institution equipped to mete justice to the righteous and punishment to the corrupt. It is just another method of conflict resolution. It may be the least just and most expensive of all the available methods. Try communication, mediation, and arbitration before adjudication.

1153. 3rd Lawyer Rule: If you are the 3rd lawyer on a case, you are the second lawyer too many.

1154. A great deal of the pressure you feel can be relieved by rehearsing what you are attempting to accomplish by giving you more confidence and control.

1155. When one door closes, another door opens; but we so often look so long and regretfully upon the closed door, that we do not see the ones, which open for us. Alexander Graham Bell

1156. Parents may enter a custody battle as a result of failed negotiation; however, a custody battle may be necessary for negotiation to begin.

1157. It is dangerous to be right when your government is wrong. Voltaire

1158. There are really only four or five set arguments you keep having with the other parent. To stop this negative pattern, list the arguments on paper. Then script them out by writing down, what they usually say, what you always answer and, what they always say back. Now you can prepare some new answers that will defuse the problem. Keep your answers polite and short. Let the other parent know you will make contact for an appointment to discuss any problems that should not be discussed in the presence of the children.

1159. Do not make excuses for yourself or the other parent.

1160. He who has begun a task has half done it. Horace

1161. Get your facts first, and then you can distort them as much as you please. Mark Twain

1162. Nothing is so exhausting as indecision, and nothing is so futile. Bertrand Russell

1163. Do not flaunt or apologize for your successes in custody court.

1164. If we could read the secret history of our enemies, we should find in each life, sorrow and suffering enough to disarm all hostility. Longfellow

1165. Today, when fear starts to grip you, feel love and joy instead.

1166. We do not lie because the truth is difficult to see. It is visible at a glance. We lie because this is more comfortable.

1167. If you cannot change a situation, you must change how you look at the situation.

1168. The shoe that fits one person pinches another; there is no recipe for living that suits all cases. Carl Jung

1169. You know you lied. They know you lied. You know they know you lied.

1170. Correct old lies as soon as possible. Do not create new lies to explain old lies.

1171. If tempted to reveal a tale someone has told about another, make it pass before you speak, through three gates of gold: First, 'Is it true?' Second, 'Is it needful?' Third, 'Is it kind?' And if to reach your lips at last it passes through these gateways three, then you may tell the tale, nor fear what the result of speech may be. Beth Day

1172. Sufficient to the day are the duties to be done and the trials to be endured. God never built a Christian strong enough to carry today's duties and tomorrow's anxieties piled on top of them.

1173. Engage your child in conversation. Listen to what your child says. Start conversations with "Tell me about, this picture you made, your day, what you want to do."

1174. The outcome of researching any legal point can only be to make two questions grow where only one grew before.

1175. As an adult it is your responsibility to know when the proverbial poop is about to hit the fan. And because no one else is able to or willing to, you owe it to everyone involved to turn off the fan.

1176. Stop whining.

1177. A duty dodged is like a debt unpaid; it is only deferred, and we must come back and settle the account at last. Joseph F. Newton

1178. When you see a turtle sitting' on a fence post, you may not know how it got there, but you can be darn sure it had help.

1179. Do not do things half way. If it is right, do it boldly - if it is wrong, leave it alone.

1180. Parents Prayer: Dear Lord, today I did what was right, I did what I had to, I did what I could, so I will not worry about the rest. It's out of my hands.

1181. There is no emotional healing in extending the emotional conflict from your daily battle to your child custody case.

1182. It is just as hard to do your job when men are sneering at you as when they are shooting at you. Woodrow Wilson

1183. Anger does as much damage to the vessel it is stored in as it does to anything it is poured upon.

1184. In Germany, they first came for the communists, and I did not speak up because I wasn't a communist. Then they came for the Jews, and I did not speak up because I wasn't a Jew. Then they came for the trade unionists, and I did not speak up because I wasn't a trade unionists. Then they came for the Catholics, and I did not speak up because I was a Protestant. Then they came for me --- and by that time no one was left to speak up. Pastor Martin Niemoller

1185. Always be polite. Always.

1186. Take responsibility that while you may not have been able to change the course of actions that lead to this child custody action, you can enhance the relationship with your children and other people you love from this point forward.

1187. About half your troubles come from wanting your way; the other half come from getting it.

1188. Every tomorrow has two handles. You can take hold of anxiety or hope. What you choose will dictate the day.

1189. Pressing points in court is the process of going up alleys to see if they are blind.

1190. Parent a lot and do it well.

1191. That which you fear confronting the most should be what you confront first.

1192. Nobody has the right to wreck your day, let alone your life. And guess what? Nobody does, you do. Gary W. Fenchuk

1193. Choose love over fear.

1194. Time is a tailor specializing in alterations.

1195. Care. Act. Speak up. Vote.

1196. You cannot plow a field by turning it over in your mind. You have to get off your butt and do something! Dail C. West

1197. The truth is, that those who have never entered family court in the pursuit of justice do not know the chaos by which they are surrounded.

1198. Who Makes The Laws? Well, you do. Either by your ignorance or indifference of what is being done, or by your active participation. You and your children have been victimized by the laws others have passed. Fight your custody battle within the confines of the existing laws. You cannot wage two wars at once. When your case is finished or reaches a stable point, go back and make the laws do what they are supposed to do. Protect our children.

1199. Once in a century a child may be ruined or made insufferable by praise. But surely, once a minute a child dies for want of it.

1200. Do not discredit the other parent, to the children.

1201. God made men big and strong so we wouldn't have to be afraid of women; it didn't work. - PC Seldom

1202. Do not say you do not have enough time. You have the same number of hours each day as Pasture, Michelangelo, Leonardo da Vinci, and Albert Einstein.

1203. Failure is never a person.

1204. Every normal man must be tempted, at times, to spit on his hands, hoist the black flag, and begin slitting throats. H.L. Mencken

1205. You'll make better progress if you'll get out of your own way.

1206. Make today better.

1207. Avoid, as you would a pestilence, two things: fear and anger. Scientific investigation has proven that these two excesses produce poisons in the body that destroy its health and break down its efficiency.

1208. Law, by itself, cannot supply us with justice. It can show us how to achieve a given end, and it may show that some ends cannot be achieved.

1209. The best preparation for the future court date is the present well seen to, and the last duty done.

1210. The fear of loss keeps us from trying, not of winning.

1211. Think about the most wonderful things you have and how hard you would work for them if you did not already have them.

1212. I have lost more in this life as a result of my fear, by wondering what might go wrong, than I will ever gain.

1213. It was not raining when Noah built the ark.

1214. Remember to thank those who help you in your struggles. The greatest humiliation in life is to work hard on something from which you expect great appreciation, and then fail to get it. Edgar W. Howe

1215. Visitation Is A Right Of The Child.

1216. Opportunity may knock just once, but temptation is a frequent visitor.

1217. It is not the critics who will be called champions, but the men in the arena, covered with mud and blood. Teddy Roosevelt

1218. The love your child has for you is in the moment you spend with the child; it is neither lost in yesterday nor does it crave for tomorrow, you child's love is now.

1219. Family Law may best be described as the art of systematic over complication.

1220. Do the right thing now.

1221. You can avoid having ulcers by adapting to the situation. If you fall in a mud puddle, check your pockets for fish.

1222. Share your wisdom - not your prejudices.

1223. Every life has its dark and cheerful hours. Happiness comes from choosing which to remember.

1224. Love is when you do not have to be with your children to touch them.

1225. I know that you believe that you understood what you think I said, but I am sure you realize that what you heard is not what I meant. Robert McCloskey, United States, State Department spokesperson.

1226. The rascals will exhaust themselves with frustration. And you will always rest well.

1227. Fanatics need not enlist. This war is crazy enough.

1228. Helpfulness is not helpful if it consists of meddling in other people's business, by volunteering, unasked, or your opinion of how they should lead their lives.

1229. When you are experiencing pain purposely or inadvertently inflicted, do something constructive for your custody case. This will minimize the emotional damage.

1230. I am only one, but I am one. I cannot do everything, but, I will not let what I cannot do interfere with what I can do. Edward Hale

1231. Custody litigants learn less from success than they do from failure.

1232. The price we pay when pursuing any art or calling is an intimate knowledge of its ugly side. James Baldwin

1233. Keep house rules, such as bedtime as consistent as possible for both homes.

1234. Say what you will about the Ten Commandments, you must always come back to the pleasant fact that there are only ten of them. H.L. Mencken

1235. Parents who live in fear limit their activities. Failure is the only opportunity to more intelligently begin again.

1236. The strongest wall between children and drugs are parents who care.

1237. The trouble with most of us is that we would rather be ruined by praise than saved by criticism. Norman Vincent Peal

1238. If we do not change direction, we arrive at where we are going. Richard E. Evans

1239. A non custodial parent may have a conscience, but no power in court. The court has power, but no conscience.

1240. Love isn't love until it is given away.

1241. Two-step formula for handling stress. Step 1. Do not sweat the small stuff. Step 2. Remember, it is all small stuff.

1242. When you say, "I love you", mean it.

1243. You must do the thing you cannot do. Eleanor Roosevelt

1244. Be prepared to compromise. No final judicial decree will be exactly what you want it to be, and there will be times when you simply must compromise for the sake of your children.

1245. If the children live in more than one home, many favorite toys will need to be duplicated.

1246. The best day, Today.

1247. The best town, Where you succeed.

1248. The best play, Work.

1249. The best work, Work you like.

1250. The cheapest, easiest and most stupid thing to do, Find fault.

1251. The greatest puzzle, Life.

1252. The cleverest person, One who always does what he thinks is right.

1253. The greatest bore, One who keeps talking after he has made his point.

1254. The greatest mystery, Death.

1255. The greatest comfort, The knowledge that you have done your work well.

1256. The best teacher, One who makes you want to learn.

1257. The greatest need, Common sense.

1258. The greatest secret of production, Saving waste.

1259. The most agreeable companion, One that would not have you any different than you are.

1260. The greatest invention of the devil, War.

1261. The most disagreeable person, The complainer.

1262. The greatest deceiver, One who deceives himself.

1263. The greatest mistake, Giving up.

1264. The meanest feeling, Envious of another's success.

1265. The most ridiculous asset, Pride.

1266. The most dangerous person, A liar.

1267. The most expensive indulgence, Hate.

1268. The biggest fool, The child who will not go to school.

1269. The worst bankrupt, The soul who has lost enthusiasm.

1270. The most important thing, Love of family, friends and self.

1271. Give people more than they expect and do it cheerfully.

1272. We are all in the gutter, but some of us are looking at the stars. Oscar Wilde

1273. Weak, is a person who permits his thoughts to control his actions; strong, is a person who forces his actions to control his thoughts.

1274. Let us not look back in anger, nor forward in fear, but around in awareness. James Thurber

1275. The meanest, most contemptible kind of praise to give is that which first speaks well to a child, and then qualifies it with a but.

1276. To get through a battle relatively unscathed, you need the strength that comes from a clear conscience and moral certainty.

1277. Everyone must row with the oars one has.

1278. I am only one; but still I am one. I cannot do everything, but still I can do something; I will not refuse to do the something I can do. Helen Keller

1279. Help other parents going through the same trials you experienced. Join parent's rights groups. It will help you, and give you a socially correct outlet to talk about separation, divorce and custody.

1280. It is possible to train a Rat! It can take years of work, years of patience, but it is possible to train a Rat. Of course, all you have then is a Trained Rat! Brother Theodore

1281. Do not let what you cannot do interfere with what you can do.

1282. Attend every occasion that the children or you feel is important. Such events are graduations, religious occasions, family events, tournaments, awards, weekly sporting events or ceremonies, recitals, even if you would rather avoid the other parent or their family. Most of these events are once in a lifetime for a child and important memories. Be there and make it happy for the child and as easy for the other parent as possible. If your obvious attendance will cause a big commotion, make a point of not being obvious. Take photos of your child so you can demonstrate to the child and others, if necessary, that you were there.

1283. You have 168 hours a week to spend.

1284. They can turn out to be the best friends you ever had, or your greatest trial. Their visits may bring joy or pain. However, they are your children's grandparents, aunts, and uncles. They are family.

1285. If it is to be, it is up to me.

1286. The way your children see their parents fight is the way your grandchildren will be watching their parents fight. If parents can learn to resolve their fights in some basically fair way, they have given their children a present, a gift, to be able to carry on to their relationships in the future. Ron Taffel

1287. Never fight a battle if you do not gain anything by winning.

1288. The chain of wedlock is so heavy that it takes two to carry it - and sometimes a judge to break it.

1289. To keep a discussion from turning into an argument, replace your use of the word "but", with the word "and".

1290. Most of the heartaches and hardships you feel your children are facing are a by-product of your unresolved fears.

1291. The road to success is always under construction, and is littered with parking places.

1292. What you dislike in another, take care to correct in yourself. Thomas Sprat

1293. Do not hold the delusion that your advancement is accomplished by crushing others. Marcus Tullius Cicero

1294. What we call failure is not the falling down, but the staying down. Mary Pickford

1295. It is an ironic habit of human beings to run faster when we have lost our way. Rollo May

1296. We must be patient - making peace is harder than making war. Adlai Stevenson

1297. Our greatest glory is not in never failing but in rising up every time we fail. Ralph Waldo Emerson

1298. You can force a herd to follow a plan of action; but, you can't force them to understand it.

1299. The Judge is just doing a job. Good or Bad, it is just a job.

1300. To forgive prior grievance has nothing to do with religion. Holding painful recollections limits your options. It is about regaining your own freedom.

1301. You have to go back a few steps to get a better jump forward.

1302. Contrary to what most people think, you are not remembered by what you did in the past, but by what most people think you did.

1303. If you find some happiness inside yourself, you'll start finding' it in a lot of other places, too.

1304. Trust but Verify.

1305. A hundred years from now, it will not matter what my bank account was, the sort of house I lived in, or the kind of car I drove. But the world may be different because I was important in the life of a child. Kathy Davis

1306. You may be deceived if you trust too much; but, you will live in torment if you don't trust enough. Frank Crane

1307. Never get vengeance and justice mixed up.

1308. Hey Jude, don't make it bad. Take a sad song and make it better. Remember to let her into your heart, then you can start to make it better. John Lennon/Paul McCartney

1309. Vision: the art of seeing things invisible. Jonathan Swift

1310. Don't believe all you hear, spend all you have, or sleep all you want.

1311. Our life is frittered away by detail. Simplify, simplify. Thoreau

1312. I am not a has-been. I am a will be. Lauren Bacall

1313. Whatever you think, feel, question, or believe is acceptable. Do not make excessive demands or impose ridged restrictions on yourself or your loved ones. Communicate tolerance, compassion and love. Live through your grief. As you slowly heal, work for balance in yourself in your permanently changed world.

1314. The best things in Life are not things. Art Buchwald

1315. Your goals should always be worthy of your efforts.

1316. Sometimes I go about in pity for myself, and all the while a great wind is bearing me across the sky. Ojibwa Saying

1317. Do not spend a $1.00 worth of time on a $.10 decision.

1318. Fear is the illusion that creates the feeling of separateness - the false sense of isolation that exists only in your imagination.

1319. Change the changeable. Accept the unchangeable. Remove yourself from the unacceptable.

1320. It's your army, impose censorship.

1321. If you do not know exactly what you want, you will not know when you have achieved it.

1322. Convincing yourself that a bad idea is a good one, is a bad idea.

1323. Getting past your anger is harder than learning to walk again.

1324. Our real blessings often appear to us in the shapes of pains, losses and disappointments; but let us have patience, and we soon shall see them in their proper figures. Joseph Addison

1325. If you do not profit from you mistakes, someone else will.

1326. When you find yourself in over your head, don't open your mouth. Swim!

1327. When you say, “I'm sorry”, look the person in the eye.

1328. The one thing that does not abide by majority rule is a person's conscience. Harper Lee

1329. Burnout can be avoided by going out and resuming social contacts. This does not mean that you have abandoned your children. It does mean that you are attempting to maintain the balance necessary for a normal life. Maintain whatever contact with your children you have been allowed.

1330. Say no to drama. Be OK with quite time.

1331. To assure yourself a good night's sleep plan your next day before retiring. First thing in the morning, review your priorities for the day.

1332. Absence of evidence, is not evidence of their absence.

1333. I have learned from experience that the greater part of our happiness or misery depends on our dispositions and not on our circumstances. Martha Washington

1334. Act the way you want to be remembered.

1335. Learn to listen. Opportunity could be knocking at your door very softly. Frank Tyger

1336. Our prime purpose in this life is to help others. And if you cannot help them, at least do not hurt them. The Dalai Lama

1337. Forget about keeping track of which clothes belong at which house.

1338. Do not take sides or take issue with decisions or actions made by the other parent, especially in front of the children.

1339. There are approximately 896,121 ways to say no. It is still no!

1340. The greater the obstacle, the more glory in overcoming it. Moliere

1341. Everyone needs recognition for his accomplishments, but few people make the need known quite as clearly as the little boy who said to his father: Let's play darts. I'll throw and you say 'Wonderful!' Grandma Moses

1342. Anybody who thinks they know everything ain't been around long enough to know anything.

1343. We must learn to live together as brothers or perish together as fools. Martin Luther King, Jr.

1344. If you were going to die soon and had only one phone call you could make, who would you call and what would you say? And why are you waiting? Stephen Eleven

1345. One of the major problems with being an attorney is that you have an obligation to observe a client's wishes, even when they seem not in the client's own interests.

1346. Poor is a state of mind. Broke is a temporary condition.

1347. And when the night is cloudy there is still a light that shines on me, Shine on until tomorrow, Let it be. John Lennon/Paul McCartney

1348. You have only one life. You can spend it laughing or crying.

1349. You do not get to choose how you are going to die or when. You can only decide how you are going to live.

1350. The only way to get out of from between a rock and a hard place is to go through it.

1351. Failure to prepare is preparing to fail. Luck is labor under knowledge.

1352. Do not allow your children to refuse visitation with the other parent.

1353. Obstacles don't have to stop you. If you run into a wall, don't turn around and give up. Figure out how to climb it, go through it, or work around it. Michael Jordan

1354. Never let yesterday use up too much of today. Will Rogers

1355. Quiet people usually know that silence is a greater obstacle than muscle.

1356. The first rule of verbal engagement is, Never argue with an idiot.

1357. Failure is never as painful or lasting as regret.

1358. Sharing, magnifies enjoyment and increases your energy.

1359. The court tries the case and the case tries the court.

1360. Scientists have proven that you cannot feel bad at the same time you are doing something nice for someone else.

1361. Once you know where you're goin', just climb in the saddle and stay on the trail 'til you get there.

1362. Learn to prioritize and compromise. Do the most important things first, but be sure they are important. Are clean clothes more important than floors you can eat off of? Then skip the mopping and do a load of laundry instead.

1363. Smile. Because no one else can do this for you.

1364. Do not plan visitation with your children, and then arrive late or not at all.

1365. Our lives begin to end the day we become silent about the things that matter. Martin Luther King

1366. If your children live in a different city than you do, subscribe to the local newspaper in their town. It will help you keep up with what is happening around them.

1367. Do not allow your teenage children to become too parental.

1368. From now on, no one will ever frighten or control me. No one will stop me from living to the fullest and loving to the fullest. Loving everyone I know and everyone I do not know, fighting for justice without seeing anyone as an enemy. David Dangler

1369. Fear less, hope more; Whine less, breathe more; Talk less, say more; Hate less, love more; And all good things are yours.

1370. Every person's custody story has value-even if only to serve as a bad example.

1371. A person's perception is reality to him.

1372. Every parent is responsible for his life's circumstances and experiences into success-no other person, and certainly, no attorney can do for a parent what he neglects to do for himself.

1373. There is nothing like winning the game to silence the critics. John Madden

1374. No single effort, no matter how mighty, will solve all of your problems. Be ambitious in your efforts to accomplish all of your goals both small and large.

1375. Ideas are great; actions are greater.

1376. Do not withhold time with the other parent as punishment for the children or the other parent.

1377. If the world is a stage, then enjoy the applause, deal with the criticism, but be aware of the torpedoes.

1378. Lawyers are paid to learn form the mistakes of others.

1379. Rudeness is the weak person's imitation of strength.

1380. Blessed is he who expects nothing, for he shall never be disappointed. Jonathan Swift

1381. Every evening try to give your child undivided attention, say for about 20-25 minutes. Turn on the phone's answering machine and allow no distractions. Set the timer and let him know that is his time and when the buzzer goes off, you are doing something else.

1382. Do not make children responsible for your or the other parent's stability.

1383. The art of becoming wise is the art of knowing what to overlook. William James

1384. Some attorneys have solutions for which there are no problems.

1385. No person is an empty vessel. Everyone fills their lives with something. It might be God, greed, revenge or love. Whatever you place in your thoughts you run toward. Commit to high ideals. Your life is worth a noble motive.

1386. Do we hate our enemies more than we love our children?

1387. When you say, I am sorry, mean it.

1388. Courage is acting even when you are filled with fear. If the challenge is important to you, you are supposed to be nervous. We only worry about the things we care about. Be brave.

1389. Reality is whatever doesn't go away when you stop believing in it. Philip K Dick

1390. Sustained efforts DO count.

1391. It has been said there are three paths to immortality: Plant a tree. Raise a child. Write a book.

1392. Do not discuss any of the financial aspects of the process (support, maintenance, arrearage) with the children.

1393. Human beings, who are almost unique in having the ability to learn from the experience of others, are also remarkable for their apparent disinclination to do so. -- Douglas Adams

1394. It ain't as bad as you think; it will look better in the morning.

1395. To be persuasive, we must be believable. To be believable, we must be credible. To be credible, we must be truthful. Edward R. Marrow

1396. You cannot make someone else's choices. You should not let someone else make yours.

1397. As your attorney, it is my duty to inform you that it is not important that you understand what I'm doing or why you're paying me so much money. What's important is that you continue to do so. Hunter S. Thompson's Samoan Attorney

1398. First, we know something with our minds (logic/ideas). Then we come to know it with our hearts (emotion/values). Later, we reveal what we know through our behavior (deeds/character).

1399. Believe nothing, no matter where you read it, or who said it - even if I have said it - unless it agrees with your own reason and your own common sense. Guatama Buddha

1400. If a person insults you to your face and then, when you are hurt, insults you again by inquiring whether or not you believe in honesty. They are more cruel than honest.

1401. Honesty is the best policy, although sometimes keeping your mouth shut is even better.

1402. Do not use the children as pawns to express anger toward the other parent.

1403. Every time you meet a situation, though you think at the time it is an impossibility and you go through the tortures of the damned, once you have met it and lived through it, you find that forever after you are freer than you were before. Eleanor Roosevelt

1404. People who neglect their obligations and responsibilities as parents are not entitled to their rights as parents.

1405. Learn what is true in order to do what is right. Thomas Henry Exile

1406. Do not overload your children by making them the focus of arguments between you and the other parent.

1407. In the end, the only thing we can bring with us is the love we leave behind.

1408. I am responsible. When you begin with these words, you can build a new life, even a new world. Know who is responsible.

1409. It is surprising what parents can do when they have to, and how little most parents will do when they do not.

1410. Experience is the worst teacher. It always gives the test first and then the instructions.

1411. People tend to behave the way you expect them to in direct ratio to your certainty and their own insecurity.

1412. Do not give in to your child's every whim. This leads to more and more time consuming battles over control. You are the parent, and your word is final.

1413. If you can be discouraged from your goals, you should be discouraged.

1414. Don't judge people by their relatives.

1415. We are all manufacturers - some make good, others make trouble and still others make excuses.

1416. Never attribute to evil what can be satisfactorily explained by stupidity.

1417. Self-advocacy begins by understanding that rights are never bestowed; they are claimed. Tony Coelho

1418. You are surrounded by so great a cloud of witnesses.

1419. Do not let your children observe sexually intimate behavior between you and your partner. Do not engage in sexually intimate behavior when your children are sleeping in the same room, even if the children's bed is screened from your bed.

1420. The meaning of things lies not in the things themselves, but in our attitude towards them. Anteing de Saint Exupery

1421. If you do not take a winning case to court you will not find one when you get there.

1422. Sometimes it's worse to win a fight than to lose. Billie Holiday

1423. Do not allow your children to sleep in the same bed with you, except for occasional, unusual circumstances.

1424. Recognize that some of your time will be spent in activities out of your control. Getting upset while waiting in traffic or sitting in a doctor's waiting room, is a waste of time. Show your children how to turn this into a time to relax or plan things you would not normally do.

1425. Do not require children to take too much responsibility for their own care.

1426. I never gave anyone hell. I just told the truth and they thought it was hell. Harry Truman

1427. Encourage your children not to keep secrets from the other parent.

1428. Politically Correct. Dishonest - ethically disoriented

1429. Help your children to value diversity. If they learn to cherish and learn from the differences among people their lives will be richer and happier.

1430. Live in the present. Do not use the past as an excuse for how to act or think.

1431. Beware of advisors that encourage you to be, or give you permission to take advantage, or be cruel. You will cause your children and yourself more pain than the target of your anger.

1432. Only the weak are cruel. Gentleness can only be expected from the strong. Leo Buscaglia

1433. You may have to fight a battle more than once to win it.

1434. Anger is a wind which blows out the lamp of the mind.

1435. Many people confuse bad planning with destiny.

1436. A client must remember that it is a lawyer's nature and duty to protect the client from anyone that can do harm including the client. Lawyers tend to be conservative and think that every course of action could lead to disaster.

1437. Little lies are usually concocted to cover up big lies.

1438. The tribal wisdom of the Lakota (Sioux) Indians, passed on from generation to generation, says that, when you discover that you are riding a dead horse, the best strategy is to dismount.

1439. It takes the same amount of time to wish as to plan.

1440. Who then can so softly bind up the wound of another as he who has felt the same wound himself? Thomas Jefferson

1441. The lawyer's first function should be to ground the client's flights of fancy and temper the client's hopes with a bracing dose of reality.

1442. Best interest of the child is usually not fair to the parents.

1443. If your child is away, do not let a phone call away be farther away than you are willing to go.

1444. What we hope to do with ease, we must learn first to do with diligence. Samuel Johnson

1445. Do not try to save the world by loving thy neighbor; it will only make him nervous. Save the world by respecting thy neighbor's rights under the law and insisting that he respect yours. E.B. White

1446. The only ZEN you find on the tops of mountains is the ZEN you bring up there. Robert M. Pirsig

1447. It is better to be alone than to wish you were alone.

1448. If you cannot write it and sign it, do not say it.

1449. Do not introduce your children to every person you date.

1450. I never take advice from my fears. General George Patton

1451. Budget for visits. No matter what the reason for the distance. It is the parents' responsibility to make sure enough money is saved for bus, train, or plane fares.

1452. In disagreements, fight fairly. No name calling.

1453. Is this pain self inflicted?

1454. Life is the first gift. Love is the second gift. Understanding is the third.

1455. Knowledge has always been one of the three tools of power: the other two are violence and wealth. Alvin Toffler

1456. The door to your cage is open. All you have to do is walk out, if you dare. George Locus, filmmaker

1457. If you sense calm, it is only because you are in the eye of the storm. Tom Peters

1458. Hurt you? Sometimes they can only do it with your help.

1459. When you lose, don't lose the lesson.

1460. Get mad, then get over it.

1461. Courage, real courage, is no quick fix. It doesn't come in a bottle or a pill. It comes from discipline, from taking everything life hands you and being your best either because of it or in spite of it. Ty Murray

1462. In the Far East the people plant a tree called the Chinese bamboo. During the first four years they water and fertilize the plant with seemingly little or no results. Then the fifth year they again apply water and fertilizer - and in five weeks' time the tree grows ninety feet in height! The obvious question is: did the tree grow ninety feet in five weeks, or did it grow ninety feet in five years? The answer is it grew ninety feet in five years. Because if at any time during those five years the people had stopped watering and fertilizing the tree, it would have died. Results in child custody court are just like that.

1463. Remember the three R's: Respect for self; Respect for others; Responsibility for all your actions.

1464. Don't let a little dispute injure a great friendship.

1465. Do not be afraid to take a big step if one is indicated. You cannot cross a chasm in two small jumps. David Lloyd George

1466. When you realize you've made a mistake, take immediate steps.

1467. Smile when picking up the phone. The caller will hear it in your voice.

1468. Marry a man/woman to whom you love to talk. As you get older, their conversational skills will be as important as any other.

1469. Open your arms to change, but don't let go of your values.

1470. "If all my talents and powers were taken from me by some inscrutable Providence, and I had my choice of keeping but one, I would choose to keep the Power of Communication, for through it, I would quickly recover all the rest." Daniel Webster

1471. Live a good, honorable life. Then when you get older and think back you'll get to enjoy it a second time.

1472. There are some who bear a grudge even to those that do them good.

1473. The most dangerous of all falsehoods is a slightly distorted truth. G. C. Lichtenberg

1474. When dealing with the other parent, reduce the volume of your voice and change your body posture.

1475. Life shrinks or expands in proportion to one's courage. Anais Nin

1476. Turn chores, such as cleaning your child's room, into quality time. Do it together and make it fast and fun.

1477. If you sit on the tracks just ignoring the facts, then don't blame the wreck on the train.

1478. When we try to pick out anything by itself, we find it hitched to everything else in the universe. John Muir

1479. Never laugh at anyone's dreams.

1480. Since then, everything has changed and changed again. And when it changed again, it did not change back.

1481. Remember that the best relationship is one where your love for each other is greater than your need for each other.

1482. If you have custody of the children and the other parent does not get to see them often, call the other parent and arrange to take the children to the other parent's job during lunch time with a picnic lunch.

1483. The only thing you know for certain is you never know. David Lee Roth

1484. When someone says, "That is a good question," the question is sure to be better than the answer you are going to get.

1485. Trust in God, but lock your car.

1486. Join the frequent flyer clubs offered by the airlines to help with the burden of long distance visitation.

1487. A loving atmosphere in your home is so important. Do all you can to create a tranquil harmonious home.

1488. In disagreements with loved ones, deal with the current situation. Don't bring up the past.

1489. Read between the lines.

1490. Share your knowledge. It's a way to achieve immortality.

1491. Pray. There's immeasurable power in it.

1492. Never interrupt when you are being flattered.

1493. Mind your own business.

1494. Don't trust a man/woman who doesn't close his/her eyes when you kiss.

1495. Once a year, go someplace you've never been before.

1496. If you make a lot of money, put it to use helping others while you are living. That is wealth's greatest satisfaction.

1497. Learn the rules then break some.

1498. Judge your success by what you had to give up in order to get it.

1499. Play cards or a board game with your children.

1500. Remember that your character is your destiny.

1501. Approach love and cooking with reckless abandon.

1502. No person is your enemy. No person is your friend. Every person is your teacher.

1503. When faced with a difficult person; you can suffer, leave, or change your internal reaction, attitude and behavior.

1504. Love deeply and passionately. You might get hurt, but it's the only way to live life completely.

1505. When the court knocks you flat on your back, remember it leaves you looking up.

1506. The Devil hath the power to assume a pleasing shape. Hamlet

1507. Do not over react to most of the bad things the children say about the other parent.

1508. No matter how much debate occurs the truth is not necessarily reached. James A. Gould

1509. Write a family history. Be truthful, yet be kind. You can learn about yourself by writing about your ancestors. When you explore their challenges and happiness's you will see many of the traits that make you the way you are. Your children will feel more connected to you as they learn about their family.

1510. The opposite of love is indifference.

1511. When someone asks you a question you don't want to answer, smile and ask, "Why do you want to know?"

1512. At some point you have to give up all hope for better yesterdays.

1513. Call your mom.

1514. Of all tyrannies, a tyranny sincerely exercised for the good of its victims, may be the most oppressive. It may be better to live under robber barons than under omnipotent moral busybodies. The robber baron's cruelty may sometimes sleep, his cupidity may at some point be satiated; but those who torment us for their own good will torment us without end, for they do so with the approval of their own conscience. C.S. Lewis

1515. We are each of us angels with only one wing, and we can only fly by embracing one another.

1516. Remember that great love and great achievements involve great risk.

1517. There is no better time or place than here. When your there, has become the here, you will simply obtain another, there, that will again look better than here.

1518. Success is the quality of your journey.

1519. I know you believe you understand what you think you heard; but I'm not sure you realize that what you heard was not what I meant.

1520. Our laws are made for moral and religious people. They are wholly inadequate for the governance of any others.

1521. Be a person of integrity - the rarest kind of human.

1522. So, I close in saying that I might have had a bad break, but I have an awful lot to live for. Lou Gehrig

1523. To cut down on the "I want" ordeal at Christmas time, throw out the catalogs before the kids see them. Restrict commercial TV, especially in December. Rent videos instead.

1524. Courage is not defined by those who fought and did not fall, but by those who fought, fell, and rose again.

1525. In dwelling live close to the ground; In thinking keep to the simple; In conflict be fair and generous; In work do what you enjoy; In family be completely present. Tai Te Ching

1526. If you want to do something positive for your children, try to improve your relationship with the other parent.

1527. You said you would do anything for your children. What your children want and need, is for you to do whatever it takes to get along with their other parent.

1528. Some people would rather relive the certainty of unhappy yesterdays than take a chance on the unknown tomorrows that could be happy.

1529. If you want to cheer yourself up, you should try cheering someone else up.

1530. It is much easier for others to suggest solutions when they know nothing about the problem.

1531. Silent company is often more healing than words of advice.

1532. Wherever you go, the world's worst drivers will have followed you there.

1533. If someone says something unkind about you, you must live so that no one will believe it.

1534. There are people who love you dearly, but just don't know how to show it.

1535. You can make someone's day by simply sending them a little note.

1536. The greater a person's sense of guilt, the greater his need to cast blame on others.

1537. You can tell a lot about a person by the way they handle these three things: a rainy day, lost luggage, and tangled Christmas tree lights.

1538. To try again, despite disappointment, is a triumph.

1539. Regardless of your relationship with your parents, you miss them terribly after they die.

1540. Making a living is not the same thing as making a life.

1541. Read more books and watch less TV.

1542. Even when you have pain, you don't have to be one.

1543. The supreme happiness of life is the conviction that we are loved. Victor Hugo

1544. Do not be afraid to spend some time alone. Do this exercise when you think everything is hopeless. List the cause of your pessimism on a sheet of paper; next to each cause, document the evidence that is real and not imagined. For each real cause, write down at least one way to counteract it.

1545. You shouldn't go through life with a catcher's mitt on both hands. You need to be able to throw something back.

1546. If anger and hate fill your heart, your brain will not be able to think clearly.

1547. Practice random acts of intelligence and senseless acts of self-control.

1548. Abandon old bad habits, focus your thoughts on positive lasting actions and chart a positive course of short and long-term goals. Avoid attempting to, "Live better by denial."

1549. If you pursue happiness, it will elude you. But if you focus on your family, the needs of others, your work, meeting new people, and doing the very best you can, happiness will find you.

1550. Whenever you decide something with kindness, you usually make the right decision.

1551. The hard thing about death is that nothing ever changes. The hard thing about life is that nothing stays the same.

1552. You can't depend on your eyes when your mind is out of focus.

1553. When an important date is coming up for someone the children love, help them make gifts for that person.

1554. You may be pulled into a "put-out-the-fire," "deal-with-the-crises" mentality. All decisions are short-term, survival based. Everything else has to be deferred until later. Life should not be deferred or endured. Life is to be lived. Find happy moments, even in "bad days."

1555. I've learned that every day you should reach out and touch someone.

1556. Unless you have a worthy long-range vision you will tend to drift and let the short-term answer or quick fix dictate your choices.

1557. Any small gesture, kindness, goal that you act upon out weighs the grandest philosophies or intentions.

1558. These are the times that try men's souls. Thomas Payne

1559. Family arguments damage children's self-esteem. Concentrate on the positive, focus on the fun and remember that the main goal isn't to get someplace or get something done. The goal is to have fun while spending quality time with your children.

1560. Learn that you still have a lot to learn.

1561. Each problem is a message stating: "What is happening does not work." It demands your attention. If you want the problem to be gone you have to find out why it is happening to you. Without looking at HOW or WHY it arose, you have done nothing to alter the underlying cause, and it will re-emerge in the same or different form over and over again.

1562. Litigation: a method for going broke methodically.

1563. Oh, what a tangled web we weave when first we practice to deceive. Sir Walter Scott

1564. Sometimes they just need a little something to make them smile.

1565. The conditions of the action are in accordance with the observations, but the observations do not agree with the effects that the actions are supposed to have given these conditions. Anonymous

1566. Reject unnecessarily negative assumptions. Keep bleak news in perspective.

1567. What you decide is less important than knowing the reasons for your decision.

1568. Hate wears you down, and does not hurt your enemy. It is like taking poison and wishing your enemy would die.

1569. When one is arguing with an idiot, it is difficult for others to discern who in fact is the idiot!

1570. It's a fact of life that we are forced to make choices we don't want to. The real test of character is not the choices we make, but how we make those choices.

1571. Recognize what has truly happened, Accept that it's over and done, and then, Take Action to Walk New Ground.

1572. If it is not right, do not do it. If it is not true, do not say it. Marcus Aurelius

1573. Right choices are easy in hindsight. But choices are actually made without hindsight, based on the information as we know it at the time.

1574. Talk slowly, but think quickly.

1575. Judge your success by what you had to give up in order to get what you wanted.

1576. Your character is your destiny.

1577. Most of all, enjoy the colorful aspects of other people's natures as long as we do not have to deal with any of the consequences.

1578. Hiroshima, Japan '1945 - Tschernobyl, Russia '1986 - You in court, Date__________ .

1579. If you can stay calm, while all around you is chaos, you probably don't completely understand the seriousness of the situation.

1580. Life sometimes gives you a second chance.

1581. Knowledge cannot come to you. You must come to knowledge.

1582. Explain your expectations for your children's behavior before you leave the house for each gathering or event.

1583. Content often follows form. It is not just that we're nice to the people we like, we like the people we're nice to.

1584. One cat at the mouse hole prevents 100 mice from entering. Sun Tsu

1585. The power to shape the future is earned through persistence. No other quality is as essential to success.

1586. Distract yourself from depressing thoughts. Every time you catch your self worrying, quickly immerse yourself in an activity that will take your mind off the troubling subject.

1587. The future you are building now is where you will be spending the rest of your life.

1588. Once you have decided someone is harmful to you, or themselves, refuse to be a supporting player in their psychodrama.

1589. Do not make a permanent decision because of a temporary situation.

1590. Respond to the problem. Do not react to the emotion.

1591. The redress of the grievances of the vanquished should precede the disarmament of the victors. Winston Churchill

1592. Turn off the radio when you are in the car with your children. It is one of the few times you will have their undivided attention. Think about the things you would like to hear about from your children. Ask about things they are interested in talking about. Avoid using this special time to lecture about problems.

1593. Do not come to a conclusion simply because you are tired of thinking.

1594. Others who disagree with us may not be wrong, bad, or evil.

1595. Mind your own business.

1596. A litigant is a red-eyed, mumbling mammal capable of conversing with inanimate objects.

1597. Everyone can use a prayer.

1598. The desires that fuel our dreams and shape our lives, flow from the attitudes we nurture every day.

1599. Poise and indifference often look the same.

1600. Chaos, panic and disorder, you are in court.

1601. Early legal advice is not expensive.

1602. An attorney's attention span is only as long as his retainer.

1603. Not all questions asked deserve an answer.

1604. Often you learn how to 'not treat people' by how you feel when people treat you badly.

1605. Take a lesson from quantum physics. When you look at something your attention or observation changes it. What you choose to notice in the people and events going on around you alters what occurs, even before you decide what response you will make. Never underestimate the power of noticing.

1606. It is a vast untidy sea of truth.

1607. Grief is the agony of an instant: the indulgence of grief, the blunder of life. Benjamin Disraeli

1608. Never match an increase in volume.

1609. People make their own history, but they do not make it under circumstances of their own choosing.

1610. All saints have a past, all sinners a future. Anton Chekov

1611. Take care of yourself so that you are neither victimized or corrupted.

1612. Examples are always wrong. But some are useful.

1613. People need and love that human touch - holding hands, a warm hug, or just a friendly pat on the back.

1614. When considering a new relationship remember how damaged your heart and mind may be. The best analogy would be that of a war damaged battleship. In the first year after a broken relationship. You will still be afloat, but listing severely to starboard, with a fire raging below decks, half the engines out of action, and half of the weapons out of service. In such a condition, going back out to "engage" isn't well on. Not until enough repairs are achieved, and the ship is again sufficiently operational to take what could come at it. If you're still in that condition, where damage control, and triage ought to be your first concern. Deal with that; then consider who you'd like to date, and where you met that type of person. Don't plan out a whole new campaign. You lost in the last one, and you need to assimilate those lessons, first.

1615. Brushing your child's hair is one of life's great pleasures. But, do not do it when you are mad at the other parent.

1616. People have a tendency to attribute meaning to words and phrases in accordance with their own beliefs and wishes. That is the phenomenon which lends a measure of semantic and pragmatic validity to words.

1617. Never let them see you sweat.

1618. The true cost of information is determined long after you buy it. You buy information with time or money. Information is power.

1619. Be a coach, not a critic.

1620. Results are the effect, caused by action. The availability of information that creates the power to act should not be evaluated on the success or acceptance of the results. Action produces more "failures" than "successes". Thomas Edison produced hundreds and thousands of results he did not want in order to get the one he did.

1621. The right decision at the wrong time is the wrong decision.

1622. For the last six months, I have been writing a book that will tell you everything I understand about my experiences in family court for the last five years - I've got the page numbers done.

1623. If you have to hide something you are doing, you are making a mistake.

1624. Get angry enough to do what it takes to reverse the losses you suffer.

1625. The two common causes of pessimism are fear and hate. The greatest danger of these emotions is that they shut off your mind.

1626. Families don't end, Marriages do.

1627. You cannot make other people do anything. You can only offer options for them to accept, modify, ignore, or decline.

1628. Do not judge the person. Judge the action of the person.

1629. One of the main jobs of consciousness is to keep our life tied together into a coherent story, a self-concept. It does this by generating explanations of behaviors on the basis of our self image, images and memories of the past, expectations of the future, the present social situation, and the physical environment in which behavior is produced. Joseph Le Doux

1630. Be aware of people who gain power through inadequacy and helplessness.

1631. Children survive in spite of and because of their parents.

1632. Your superior knowledge or greater experience does not make you a superior person, but rather a potential highly credible source of advice. But, only when asked.

1633. I offer my opponents a bargain: if they will stop telling falsehoods about us, I will stop telling the truth about them. Adlai Stevenson

1634. Big boys and girls do cry.

1635. There are people that are always sincere. They can't hold on the same point of view from one minute to the next, but they are always sincere.

1636. No longer lend your strength by word and action to that which you wish to be free from.

1637. When you find a solution to a problem, it is usually a comfortable solution. Find several other solutions. Then pick the best, not the most comfortable.

1638. Ninety-nine per cent of the people in the world are fools and the rest of us are in great danger of contagion. Thornton Wilder from The Matchmaker

1639. If you help someone up the hill, you get closer to the top yourself.

1640. Everyone has dreams for their children and for themselves. What is rare is the courage to take action and follow through.

1641. The only truth they will accept is their own.

1642. Our bodies are made of cells. Each part of our life is made up of cells. In a healthy body all of the cells are replaced every three years. The body begins to age and die when cells are not properly replaced. The same thing happens with the cells of our lives.

1643. Send your child postcards with photos that tell a story.

1644. You can't scare me - I have been to court.

1645. Only by taking the risk of going too far can we determine how far we can go.

1646. For the truly faithful, no miracle is necessary. For those who doubt, no miracle is sufficient. Nancy Gibbs

1647. Nothing in all the world is more dangerous than sincere ignorance and conscientious stupidity. MLK Jr.

1648. What one has to do usually can be done. Eleanor Roosevelt

1649. Help your children understand and support in an appropriate manner, the other parent in times of stress or loss.

1650. There will be a residue of fear and resentment as a result of the adversarial position imposed by the court proceedings. Assure the other parent that the partnership is for the child's welfare and that you will assist the parent and your child to the best of your ability. This will provide your child with a more secure environment. Two parents living apart will not see their children as much as two parents living together.

1651. Courage is like a muscle, it is strengthened by use.

1652. Good clear ice two inches thick will bear the weight of a grown person; four inches thick will bear a horse and rider; six inches thick will bear the weight of a compact car. But your skin never gets thick enough to bear an unkind word about your child.

1653. Danger lies not in what we don't know, but in what we think we know that just ain't so. Mark Twain

1654. God isn't alarmed when we hit rock bottom. He made the rock.

1655. Only the educated have power. Education can be gained in the classroom, through research or in day to day life. Gathering information, understanding what the information is telling you, then using it correctly is education.

1656. If stupidity got us into this mess, then why can't it get us out? Will Rogers

1657. The prisons of this country are littered with the bodies of good people for whom any serious crime was the farthest thought. Now they count days doing the brick yard walk because they obstructed justice or committed perjury for a friend.

1658. We would like to think that our children are only products of our parenting skills, but sometimes that is not the case. Sometimes, they become great people in spite of us.

1659. Nothing gives one person so much advantage over another as to remain always cool and unruffled under all circumstances. Thomas Jefferson

1660. To have a crisis and act upon it, is one thing. To live in perpetual crisis is another.

1661. Let your children see and hear your appreciation of all the things the other parent does for them. Compliment the other parent in an honest manner for positive behaviors and things done for the children.

1662. Truth often suffers more by the heat of its defenders, than from the arguments of its opposers. William Penn

1663. To abandon one's self to the luxury of grief: it deprives one of courage, and even of the wish for recovery. Henry Frederic Amiel

1664. For you and your children to survive a legal battle with minimum damage, you must free yourself unilaterally from the old patterns in which you and the other parent have been trapped.

1665. Give to every other human being every right you claim for yourself. Robert Green Ingersoll

1666. When wealth is lost, nothing is lost that cannot be regained; when health is lost, something is lost; when character is lost, all is lost. German Motto

1667. When you become involved in a child custody battle it is best to cross your fingers and pray to whatever gods you think might take an interest in your problems.

1668. If you cannot handle your own setbacks with grace, there is no reason to expect that your kids will. Richard Carlson

1669. The promises of the future have arrived, they are just not evenly distributed.

1670. Go, sir, gallop, and don't forget that the world was made in six days. You can ask me for anything you like except time. Napoleon

1671. Remember the game you played when you were a kid, where you passed a phrase from person to person? Usually, the words changed a lot in the retelling. Same way with gossip. What starts out one way can come around completely different.

1672. The purpose of all war is peace. Saint Augustine

1673. You may decide to put a tape recorder on your telephone. It is amazing how exquisitely polite you become when you are sure all of your telephone calls are recorded. If you are not recording your own calls, you may be sure the other side is, and you would be wise to practice using a polite tone and answer at all times.

1674. And the little screaming fact that sounds through all history; repression works only to strengthen and knit the repressed. John Steinbeck

1675. No man is above the law and no man is below it; nor do we ask any man's permission when we require him to obey it. Theodore Roosevelt

1676. Write each of your children personal letters and holiday cards.

1677. Be aware of how your words will sound out of context. Context is what you mention when you are forced to rationalize bad behavior.

1678. Create a video tour of your neighborhood, home, yard, room, doing something like a family dinner or a trip.

1679. The beginning of wisdom is to call things by their right name. Chinese Proverb

1680. Billy Joel made a song called "Second Wind". He tells us to wait for or get the second wind. Life's "on-hold" for now, that's all.

1681. All of us are subjected to somebody else's power at some point, so once in a while you kiss ass. So what? Either you make peace with that early, or you end up living your life as a crank and a misfit. Kinsey Millhone in Sue Grafton's, "H is for Homicide"

1682. If there were only one single truth, it would not be possible to paint a hundred pictures of the same subject. Picasso

1683. The soul of man is divided into three parts, intelligence, reason, and passion. Intelligence and passion are possessed by other animals, but reason by man alone. Reason is immortal, all else mortal. Pythagoras

1684. Before you run, check to see if the bulldog has teeth. Les Brown

1685. Do not confuse your child's needs with your wants.

1686. Collect stories about your parents or grandparents: make a book, illustrate with photos or drawings, for you, for your children.

1687. Knowledge will forever govern ignorance, and a people who mean to be their own governors, must arm themselves with the power knowledge gives. James Madison

1688. The law is reason unaffected by desire. Aristotle

1689. It is funny how God can forgive you and people cannot.

1690. When I ask you to listen to me and you start giving me advice, you have not done what I asked. When I ask you to listen to me and you begin to tell me why I should not feel that way, you are trampling on my feelings. When I ask you to listen to me and you feel you have to do something to solve my problem, you have failed me, strange as that may sound. Listen! All I ask is that you listen. Do not talk or do - just hear me. Author Unknown

1691. Habit is a cable; we weave a thread of it every day, and at last we cannot break it. Horace Mann

1692. Don't give up. Lot's of things look like they are spoiling just before they age to perfection.

1693. Be curious about life. Stick around to find out what's next.

1694. People make their own history, but, they do not make it under circumstances of their own choosing. Karl Marx

1695. Those who do not feel pain seldom think that it is felt. Samuel Johnson

1696. To the world you might be one person, but to one person you might be the world.

1697. Click! Click! Click! There's no place like home. Dorothy

1698. Someone lives for what you are, what you give them and for what your life means to them. Even when you are being difficult, you are still loved.

1699. Courage means putting fear aside and doing your job.

1700. There are about as many ways to improve your custody case as there are to destroy it.

1701. After court finishes, you still have to deal with the other parent.

1702. Opportunities are disguised by hard work, so most people do not recognize them. Ann Landers

1703. Before we bring you into the courtroom, I'd like to impress upon you that quality, excellence, and good taste aren't everything.

1704. Virtue is a habit and so is Vice. Cicero

1705. The light on the horizon of the new day is raw opportunity: Make something of it.

1706. Even if you are not suspicious, watch the skies as you park you car at the court house. If you see vultures circling over head, do not go in.

1707. God gives every bird his worm; but, he does not throw it into the nest. Swedish Proverb

1708. In law school, you learn that there is no right or wrong answer. There's just the best argument.

1709. With money a dragon. Without money a worm. Chinese Proverb

1710. Figure out a way to create a home, school, or work environment that is enjoyable.

1711. If you don't do what needs doing, before long you won't have the chance to do anything at all. Harry Turtledove the book Prince of the North

1712. Truth emerges more readily from error than success.

1713. You are always most surprised by your own obituary.

1714. I wonder if I'm the only parent here who observes my own behavior in my children and am shocked and dismayed by it. Sometimes, I have observed my children saying or doing something that mirrors me exactly, and seeing it from the observation of a spectator, instead of an actor. I am forced into changing my behavior and try to change the action or verbiage of the child because I don't like it as portrayed by my children.

1715. Equity: When looked for, it vanishes, when sought, it disappears.

1716. Find comparisons to people today with people in your past. If you do it honestly, and see why you invited these people into your life you will learn a great deal about yourself.

1717. People who will not reason are weak; people who cannot reason are fools; and people who dare not reason are slaves.

1718. If you think hiring an attorney with a good education and experience in domestic relations is expensive, try a cheap ignorant one.

1719. There is no sport in hate when all the rage is on one side. Percy Shelly

1720. The first principle is that you must not fool yourself and you are the easiest person to fool. Richard Feynman, one of the 20th century's great Scientists.

1721. I may make you feel, but, I can't make you think.

1722. It can take as much as five years to see, that something horrible the judge did to you, made things work out the way you wanted them to work out.

1723. The world is quickly bored by the recital of misfortune and willingly avoids the sight of distress. Sommerset Maugham

1724. They may not be bad people getting good. They may be sick people getting well.

1725. Do not hire a professional until you know what you want from that person.

1726. Consider those whom you call your enemies, and figure out what they should call you. Dwayne Dyer

1727. The bigger the why, the easier the how.

1728. If you act like a jerk when dealing with a jerk, you may be the only one remembered as a jerk.

1729. It finally happened. After a random check, the AMA and Association for Mental Health and OSHA have designated that family court is "unfit for human visitation."

1730. Words are clothes that thoughts wear. Samuel Butler

1731. Family court is the only place where people treat a court order as a suggestion.

1732. All excuses are useless.

1733. We are measured by what we finish, not what we start. Norma Howland

1734. I could never think well of a man's intellectual or moral character, if he was habitually unfaithful to his appointments. Nathaniel Emmons

1735. If you're there before it's over, you're on time. James J. Walker

1736. Punctuality is disappointing if no one is there to appreciate it.

1737. An Igni-second is the overlapping moment of time when the hand is locking the car door even as the brain is saying, “my keys are in there!” Rich Hall

1738. In the first round of work simplification ... you can reasonably expect a 30 to 50 percent reduction ... To implement the actual simplification, you must question why each step is performed. Typically, you will find that many steps exist in your work flow for no good reason. Often they are there by tradition or because formal procedure ordains it, and nothing practical ordains it. Andrew S. Grove the CEO Intel Corp

1739. Time is like money, the less we have of it to spare the further we must make it go.

1740. This court appearance, like all court appearances needs planning and preparation, to be a good one. To survive and learn the most from it we must know what the best and worst possible outcome can be.

1741. One always has time enough, if one will apply it well. Goethe

1742. Lost time with the people we love is never found again. If you cannot be with one you love, do not make the time you have with another you love miserable because of it.

1743. Our time and attention are at once the most valuable and the most perishable of all the gifts we can give our children.

1744. These times of ours are serious and full of calamity, but all times are essentially alike. As soon as there is life there is danger. Ralph Waldo Emerson

1745. A Nano-second is the shortest possible measure of time, discovered recently in family court. Generally speaking, it is the time between when something happens in your favor and everything falls apart.

1746. When you get to the end of your rope, tie a knot and hang on.

1747. If you have two equally likely solutions to a problem, pick the simplest.

1748. And the trouble is, if you do not risk anything, you risk even more. Erica Jong

1749. You can get anything you want if you help others get what they want.

1750. The tricky part of any lie is trying to figure out how you would act if you were innocent.

1751. Do not make the call to your attorney longer because you have not taken the time to think it through beforehand. Think it through and make it shorter.

1752. Any good law can be misused.

1753. Parents in a child custody battle resemble a pair of shears, so joined that they cannot be separated; often moving in opposite directions, yet always punishing anyone who comes between them.

1754. A fool in court soon becomes wise.

1755. Establish yourself as the parent seen by the child's doctor, teachers, scout leader, neighbors and minister.

1756. You can get everywhere you need to be if you take the time to plan and prepare to get there.

1757. Your life is the product of your past decisions.

1758. Settle. Settle. Settle. Settle. Settle. Settle. Settle.

1759. What gets measured, gets done.

1760. Failure is the opportunity to begin again, more intelligently. Henry Ford

1761. Today is the tomorrow you worried about yesterday.

1762. The fundamental principle of the adversary system or model is that the path to legal truth is obtained by having the two sides of the case in question draw apart the evidence-literally.

1763. Your heart, your spirit, your financial future; If it ain't broke, bring it to family court, we'll break it.

1764. A great many things are possible: but not practical. Isaac Asimov

1765. Winning a custody case doesn't change people, it only unmasks them.

1766. 90% of good parenting is just being there. Be there whenever the courts let you. Let the other parent be there whenever the other parent can. Children need as much good parenting as they can get.

1767. One does not have to apologize for or explain what one does not say.

1768. Opportunity often comes in the form of misfortune, or temporary defeat. Napoleon Hill

1769. #1. You are not responsible for other peoples' feelings or what they do. #2. You are responsible for your own feelings and your actions.

1770. The pursuit of what is possible is gratifying and healthy; the pursuit of what is not possible is frustrating, neurotic, and a terrible waste of time.

1771. Do not let the shattered dreams of yesterday blur your visions of tomorrow.

1772. The good man is the man who, no matter how morally unworthy he has been, is moving to become better. John Dewey

1773. Never take blame or credit for something you did not do.

1774. There is no failure except in no longer trying. There is no defeat except from within, no really insurmountable barrier save our own inherent weakness of purpose. Kin Hubbard

1775. The limits that matter are those you create in your mind.

1776. Hard work is often the easy work you did not do at the proper time. Bernard Meltzer

1777. Waiting is a trap. There will always be reasons to wait ... The truth is, there are only two things in life, reasons and results, and reasons simply don't count. Robert Anthony

1778. Things may come to those who wait, but only the things left by those who hustle. Abraham Lincoln

1779. Putting off an easy thing makes it hard, and putting off a hard one makes it impossible. George H. Lonmer

1780. A good manager knows that there is more than one way to skin a cat. A great manager can convince the cat that it is necessary. Gene Perret

1781. Never tell people how to do things. Tell them what to do and they well surprise you with their ingenuity. General George Patton

1782. You control your attitude or it controls you.

1783. Hire the best. Pay them fairly. Communicate frequently. Provide challenges and rewards. Believe in them. Get out of their way---they'll knock your socks off. Mary Ann Allison in "Managing Up, Managing Down"

1784. Delegation is giving people things to do. Management is accomplishing organizational goals by working through individuals and groups. It is easy to see that the two are closely entwined. And it is obvious that the manager who is not delegating is not managing. Robert Maddux

1785. Do not look for ways to change others, look for opportunities to become a better parent yourself.

1786. According to a recent issue of Psychology Today; research shows that a slight protrusion of your tongue between your lips, while you're working, is taken as an unspoken "Do Not Disturb" sign by most people. The next time you're trying to complete a file on an impossible task, you might want to try this technique. Canadian Lawyer magazine

1787. The best time for you to hold your tongue is the time you feel you must say something or bust. Josh Billings

1788. It is by presence of mind in untried emergencies that the native metal of man is tested. James Russell Lowell

1789. We must all hang together, or most assuredly we shall all hang separately. Benjamin Franklin

1790. You see the court a few times. They have seen you a thousand times.

1791. Anyone who writes, feels they can't really get it all down. But, you can. Think it through. Write it down, read it out loud to see if it says what you want it to say. And make corrections if you need to do so. Its amazing how this process clarifies your thoughts.

1792. We make way for the man who boldly pushes past us. Christian Nestell Bovee

1793. Don't fight stupid. Stupid don't fight.

1794. In order to speak short on any subject, think long. H.H. Brackenridge

1795. Imagine that every Thursday your shoes exploded if you tied them the usual way. This happens to us all the time with computers, and nobody thinks of complaining. Jeff Raskin

1796. E-mail allows attorneys to communicate on a one-to-one basis with their clients. Because some secretaries did not fix their sloppy writing, clients wonder how the attorneys passed English 101.

1797. Perhaps Hell is nothing more than a person involved in a mediation who has no intention of mediating and takes an eternity to demonstrate it.

1798. When the result of a court date is to schedule more court dates, it usually indicates trouble.

1799. Oh, I ain't worried Miss, I gave myself up for dead back where we started. Humphrey Bogart's character in the African Queen

1800. You can't effect the cards that you are dealt in life, but you can determine how you play your cards.

1801. The workers of the world will soon be divided into two distinct groups. Those who will control computers and those who will be controlled by computers. It would be best for you to be in the former group.- Lewis Eigen, 1961

1802. Telephone: An invention of the devil which abrogates some of the advantages of making a disagreeable person keep his distance. Ambrose Bierce

1803. Natives who beat drums to drive off evil spirits are objects of scorn to smart Americans who blow horns to break up traffic jams. Mary Ellen Kelly

1804. If custody was simply a matter of law, we would not be here.

1805. The pace of progress in a child custody war may be determined by the principals' acceptance or rejection of systems they view as too expensive or overly complicated.

1806. Consider the postage stamp: Its usefulness consists in the ability to stick to one thing till it gets there. J. Billings

1807. By all means, let us simplify the means of controlling time and the myriad details of our lives; but, let us vigorously preserve our responsibility to direct our lives toward human accomplishment, rather than the pure accumulation of information. Paul Rice

1808. For over a half century now I've watched office obesity develop into a full-blown, crippling disease. As our office clutter mounts, we're ever more intimidated and frustrated by it. We engineer drainage and removal of water and liquid wastes from society to prevent hazardous buildup, but the effluent that pours into our offices-paper-is never flushed out. Don Aslett

1809. Sign on cluttered desk: A clean desk may show efficiency, neatness and organization, but very seldom provides a worthwhile surprise. Charles Averson

1810. The only cure for grief is action. George Henry Lewes

1811. When dealing with the growing irritation of another person; set yourself in a protective, balanced stance. Remain as calm, polite, and flexible as possible while firmly moving toward your goal.

1812. It isn't wise to trust your entire future to any profession that a person handling the critical questions in your life must advertise that they are "practicing."

1813. It ain't the things we don't know that cause us the most trouble. It's the things we do know that ain't so.

1814. Our two greatest problems are gravity and paperwork. We can lick gravity, but sometimes the paperwork is overwhelming. Dr. Wernher Von Braun

1815. Remember that silence is sometimes the best answer.

1816. I really cannot give you the formula for success. But I can give you the formula for failure. It's this: Try to please everyone. Bernard Meltzer

1817. Unfaithfulness in the keeping of an appointment is an act of clear dishonesty. You may as well borrow a person's money as his time. Horace Mann

1818. Failing to admit that you were wrong is saying you are still wrong. Admitting you were wrong is saying I am now wiser than I was.

1819. Communicate with children that live far away using the VCR, audio tapes, and photographs when possible.

1820. Anticipate questions the other parent will ask, objections the other parent will raise, and concerns the other parent will present. Prepare appropriate responses that will allow the other side to reach the same goals that you have.

1821. Failure is not the only punishment for inaction, there is also the success of others.

1822. Do whatever is necessary to resolve angry feelings toward the other parent.

1823. We see what we believe, and not just the contrary. To change what we see, it is sometimes necessary to change what we believe. Ignore your enemy with compassion.

1824. People on this planet would come closer to finding inner peace if they would believe just two truths: (1) you cannot control other people; and (2) you can control yourself.

1825. Mind your speak. Do not speak your mind.

1826. Even the best of us can serve as horrible examples.

1827. Regardless of where you are, all recovery roads lead to a healing process sooner or later; because if you did not make a right turn, three left turns make a right ... eventually.

1828. Help your children learn how to think rather than what to think.

1829. The greatest obstacle to discovery is not ignorance, it is the illusion of knowledge. Daniel Boorstin

1830. Success is how high you bounce when you hit bottom. General George Patton

1831. Never let the fear of striking out get in your way. Babe Ruth

1832. Self-test for: Total lack of control in your life: You know you have it when you can't think of anything that's your own fault.

1833. To let go is not to deny but to accept.

1834. Forget mistakes. Forget failures. Forget injustices and pain. Forget everything except what you are going to do NOW. Then do it. Today is your lucky day.

1835. There is no security on this earth; there is only opportunity. General Douglas MacArthur

1836. The law isn't justice. It's a very imperfect mechanism. If you press exactly the right buttons and are also lucky, justice may show up in the answer. A mechanism is all the law was ever intended to be. Raymond Chandler

1837. Keep making decisions, even when they are wrong.

1838. You can't solve problems with the same type of thinking that created them. Albert Einstein

1839. You would have beat me in a fair fight, hardly gives me any incentive to fight fair, now does it?

1840. Emotions are often the most difficult thing for us to deal with. Sometimes, it's not what happens to us but how we react that determines our emotional state and ultimately our happiness or lack of. There are, of course, certainly exceptions.

1841. Lawyer syndrome - the world is black and white.

1842. With the passing of time, the aftershocks happen less often and are less intense as well.

1843. There is more hunger for love and appreciation in this world than for bread. Mother Teresa

1844. Respect, regard, restraint.

1845. Our experiences can either grind us or polish us.

1846. The basis for every decision, every event we create in our lives stems from either fear or love.

1847. You can look back now and see that the reasons were flawed and wrong, but when you remember your mindset at the time, and what you “knew” then, you will see that you could not have done anything different. No, have no regrets.

1848. Sometimes, you are not the target.

1849. Knowledge will forever govern ignorance, and a people who mean to be their own Governors, must arm themselves with the power knowledge gives. James Madison

1850. Those that accept themselves, unconditionally, seem to accept others, unconditionally. And those that don't accept themselves, unconditionally, don't accept others, unconditionally.

1851. Success is getting up one time more than you fall down.

1852. The certainty of misery is better than the misery of uncertainty. Walt Kelly's 'Pogo'

1853. We are born fearing only two things; loud sounds and falling. The rest are learned.

1854. Put a note on your mirror that says, "You are looking at the problem" put another that says, "You are also looking at the solution"

1855. No one will know you will tolerate abuse, unless you present yourself as willing to be abused.

1856. When the power of love overcomes the love of power there will be peace.

1857. The person who never wastes anything has always got something to give.

1858. Lost time is never found again.

1859. Life is too short to sit around wondering what to do.

1860. If I have to I can do anything.

1861. Those who bring sunshine into the lives of others cannot keep it from themselves.

1862. Your children will find happiness anywhere that people take the time to care.

1863. Don't be content with the what, but get to know the why and how.

1864. Very little is needed to make your life happy, it is within yourself, within your way of thinking.

1865. Don't be afraid to give some of yourself - it will all grow back.

1866. Learn from yesterday, live for today, look for tomorrow.

1867. Life is either a daring adventure or nothing.

1868. All people smile in the same language

1869. We write our own destiny ... we become what we do.

1870. It is useless to close the gates to new ideas, they simply leap over them.

1871. If you know what hurts you, you know what hurts others.

1872. Habit is more important than smart.

1873. The mind is like a parachute - it functions only when open.

1874. In Biblical times, men who wanted to care for their children were called fathers. Today, we call them child support payees.

1875. No one will know that you command and expect respect, unless you present yourself as someone who commands and expects respect.

1876. No one will know you are afraid, unless you present yourself as being afraid.

1877. No one can make you a victim, unless you present yourself as someone who can be victimized.

1878. Our lives begin to end the day we become silent about things that matter. Dr. Martin Luther King, Jr.

1879. The fact is if you are not following your own plan, you are most assuredly following someone elses.

1880. The significant problems we cannot solve at the same level of consciousness with which we created them. Albert Einstein

1881. I started with nothing. I still have most of it.

1882. The best answer to a statement to which you disagree and do not wish to debate is, "And you may most certainly think that."

1883. Don't mistake kindness for weakness.

1884. He who will not risk cannot win. Patrick Henry

1885. If you have to make a choice, but you do not, that is the choice.

1886. Courage, *real* courage, is no quick fix. It doesn't come in a bottle or a pill. It comes from discipline. From taking everything life hands you and being your best, either because of it or in spite of it. Ty Murray

1887. Each child has his or her own destiny.

1888. Success and Failure, treat both impostors just the same. Rudyard Kipling

1889. Learn the rules so you know how to break them properly.

1890. Nothing destroys a child's faith in you more completely than you breaking promises to that child.

1891. The best relationship is one in which your love for each other exceeds your need for each other.

1892. Don't just listen to what someone is saying. Listen to why they are saying it.

1893. Write a short story about a conflict you had with the other parent, told from the perspective of your child.

1894. There is no system of law in the world that guarantees the right results.

1895. Make pictures of your child's pictures. Put them together into a memory book or plaster a wall with them.

1896. This is not about you. It is about your child. Always.

Win Your Child Custody War

Expertly indexed to allow you to access the critical information you need instantly. You can't waste weeks and hundreds of dollars each time the other side drops a bomb on your case. This manual will allow you to identify, evaluate, and respond with lightning speed and effectiveness to short circuit dangerous tactics. Everyone tells you what you can't do.

Who's In Charge Of Your Child Custody Case?

- Remarkable no-nonsense method to understand and manage your case.
- When and how the court will listen to your child's wishes.
- Child's Affidavit of Preference or Choice of Managing Conservator example.
- Voluntary Relinquishment of Parental Rights and Stepparent Adoption.
- Grounds for Involuntary Termination/Relinquishment of Rights.
- Dealing with lies; theirs, yours, and the biggest lie of all.
- Example of a filed Contempt Motion and Answer.
- How and if smoking, dental neglect, drugs, abandonment, and abuse affect your case.
- When and how to use detectives and experts.
- Examples of detective assignments and final reports.

Killers and **Boosters**

- E-mail, chat rooms and computer forensics impact your case.
- The affect your case and job can have on each other.
- Evaluator reports, psychological evaluations and home studies.
- How to prepare for psychological evaluations and home study reports.
- More than 91 citing, summarizing, quotes from, reference relevant cases/decisions.
- When and how to dispose someone to get the result you need.
- How much money a custody case costs and when it is spent.
- Options for reducing the cost of your case.
- Ways to make your child kidnap resistant.
- Information a child should know if the opportunity to escape arises.
- Identify and control your own problem behaviors.
- Child support; paying it, collecting it, and changing it.
- Determine who you can talk to and what you can tell them.
- Learn about the most common situations that cause panic.
- What the situations really mean and options for handling them.
- Hire a great attorney, fire a bad one, know if you can sue a bad one.
- Why and how to keep a contact log book and when to use it.
- 640 + triple columned pages of the most valuable and up-to-date information available.

Table of Contents and Index available at http:/www.custody-war.com

The fact is if you are not following your own plan,
you are most assuredly following someone elses

How To Go To Visitation Without Throwing-Up

I have been going to visitation since I was born in October 1991. I have gotten there by car, van, 18 wheeler truck, train, taxi-cab and airplane. When I was a baby I did not care.

When I got bigger, I would cry not to go. My dad would hold me and I would shake and cry. I was not afraid of my mom, I just did not want to go away. I wanted everyone I loved to stay around me. I traveled to visitation and home 4 to 6 times a year for the big holidays, spring break and summer. Visitation has been a big thing in my life and I hope I can help you with yours. Joshua Shane Evans

See the Table of Contents at www.Joshua-Evans.com

Dear Judge,

Children's Letters to the Judge. These letters deal with Fear, Anger, Confusion, Love, Grief and Hope.

It is difficult for parents to know what children think. Often children feel helpless and only give the answers they think the grown-ups want. These letters are straight from the hearts and minds of children to the person they think can fix everything.

Witness Guide

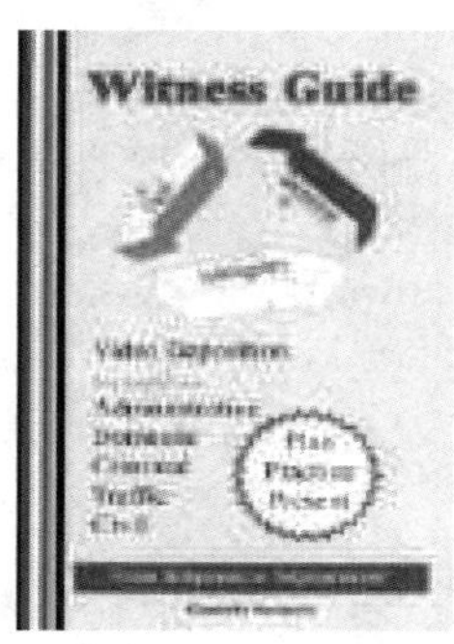

One of the biggest problems we face as litigants in a lawsuit is figuring out how to tell our side of the story. Just getting people we know to understand what we are saying is difficult, and the thought of a hostile attorney firing trick questions at us in front of others causes terror in the bravest most willing witness.